LEEDS
DESCRIB'D

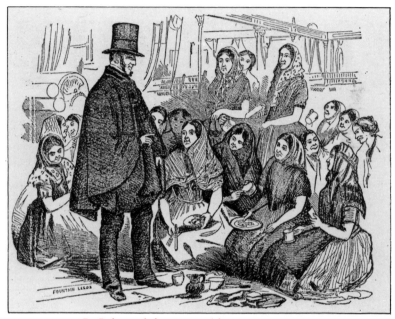

Dr Baker and the factory girls (see pages 46-8).

LEEDS DESCRIB'D

Eyewitness Accounts of Leeds
1534-1905

ANN HEAP
& PETER BREARS

The Breedon Books
Publishing Company
Derby

First published in Great Britain by
The Breedon Books Publishing Company Limited
44 Friar Gate, Derby DE1 1DA
1993

ISBN 1 873626 16 9

Printed and bound by Hillman Printers (Frome) Ltd.
Covers printed BDC Printing Services Ltd, Derby.

List of Illustrations

Cover: Watercolour of Lower Briggate before the widening of Boar Lane in 1867, by Walter Braithwaite.

Preface

1993 marks the centenary of Leeds gaining its charter as a city. Among the numerous celebrations which will take place this year is an exhibition entitled 'Leeds Describ'd', which displays a wealth of local maps, plans, books, paintings and artefacts drawn from the magnificent collections of the City Library and the City Museum.

Today Leeds is a great European city, with a growing reputation for its rich architectural and industrial heritage, its great musical and theatrical traditions, its sporting achievements, its fine central shopping area and markets, and its fine parks and woodland. All these elements play such a normal part in the lives of Leeds people, that it is very easy to take them for granted, but events such as centenaries give us the opportunity to reflect on the past, and to appreciate how much we owe to the efforts of previous generations.

In this book Ann Heap of the Local History Reference Library and Peter Brears, the Director of Museums, have drawn together a fascinating range of eye-witness accounts of Leeds as it appeared both to visitors and to 'Loiners' between 1538 and 1905. This was the major period of expansion which saw Leeds grow from a small town of low half-timbered buildings to one of the world's greatest manufacturing cities, exporting its products to every part of the known world. It should be read by all those who know Leeds today, and especially by those young people who will be responsible for maintaining its success into the future.

Cllr. Bernard Atha,
Chairman, Cultural Services Committee,
1993.

Introduction

Every year thousands of people come into the City's Local History Library and the City Museum to gather information on a vast range of subjects relating to Leeds and its region. Some come with very specific enquiries relating to a particular person, place or activity, while others are looking for general background material on such themes as 'Children in Factories', 'Victorian Leeds', etc. Fortunately Leeds has been the subject of local history research of the very highest quality for many years, from the publication of Ralph Thoresby's *Ducatus Leodiensis* in 1715 to the recent monumental works of the renowned Professor Beresford. Even so, some of the most interesting references lie scattered among travelogues, government enquiries, diaries, public health reports and other works written by a variety of authors between the sixteenth and the twentieth centuries. A selection of these have now been drawn together into this single volume, in order to make them much more accessible to the public. Where the original pieces are of great length appropriate extracts have been chosen to illustrate their more interesting points.

In these accounts we can follow the gradual progress and expansion of Leeds. During the sixteenth and seventeenth centuries, it was still a pleasant ancient market town, that 'stondith most by clothing' the local woollen industry making it 'the wealthyest town of its bigness in the Country'. The eighteenth century saw the town flourish in wealth and beauty, as the fabulous profits of the world's largest market in woollen cloth were used to finance magnificent new public buildings, churches, merchants' houses, and a cultivated and lively social scene. By the late Georgian period, however, the first signs of pollution and squallor were becoming apparent, as the town became increasingly industrialised. From then on the vast expansion of manufacturing brought with it massive environmental problems, as a pall of sulphurous smoke blotted out the sun above, foetid vapours rose from the vile blackness of the River Aire, and the streets and yards flowed with filth and excrement. The Town Council made valiant efforts to provide sanitary reforms, good education, and other improvements, but little real progress had been made by the time Leeds achieved its City status in 1893. Fortunately people with real vision and influence then began to transform the appearance of Leeds, Colonel Harding starting this progress by creating City Square as a fine Italianate piazza in 1903, for example. Since then, and particularly over the last thirty years, Leeds has changed enormously as smoke control orders, clean-up campaigns and slum clearances have rid the city of the worst symptoms of its industrial past. However, the study of Leeds history, and the observations and opinions of those who had first-hand knowledge of it in previous centuries, is still extremely rewarding.

We hope that this book will prove useful and interesting to all those who already know Leeds, to those visitors who want to discover something of its history, and to teachers, and children, especially those involved in Attainment Targets 1 to 3 of the National Curriculum, and in the study of Tudor and Stuart times, Victorian Britain and the expansion of British Trade and Industry 1750-1900.

Ann Heap & Peter Brears
Leeds, 1993.

Acknowledgements

We are most grateful for Mr R.A.F.Palmer of Robertsbridge, Sussex, to quote from the manuscript diary of Mrs Sarah Ellis, to Mr Anton Rippon of Breedon Books for his great assistance with this publication and to Mrs Gill Philipson, for typing the text.

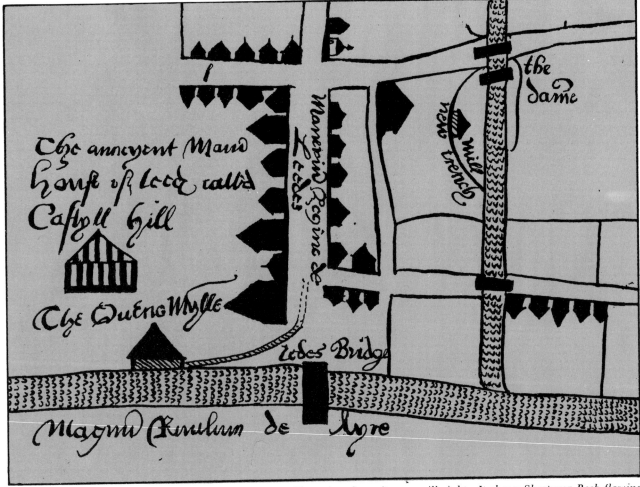

Dating from 1560, this plan of Leeds was produced as evidence in a lawsuit over mill rights. It shows Sheepscar Beck flowing down from the north to join the river Aire, which runs across the bottom of the plan. Note the houses lining Briggate just above 'Ledes Bridge', with 'The auncyent manor house of Leeds call'd Castyll Hill' to the left with 'The Quene's Mylle' below and Falkingham's Mill at Millgarth to the right.

1534

John Leland (1506-1553) became antiquary to King Henry VIII in 1553. He made a tour through England from 1534 and the notes he compiled were first published as *Leland's Itinerary* in 1710.

Ledis, 2. Miles lower than Christal Abbay on Aire Ryver, is a praty Market, having one Paroche Chirche reasonably welle buildid, and as large as Bradeford, but not to quik as it. The Toun stondith most by Clothing.

1586

William Camden (1551-1623) published the first detailed description of Britain in his *Britannia* of 1586. The following text comes from the first English translation of this work, published in 1610.
Camden, W. *Britannia* (1610) p.694

From hence *Are* passeth beside *Kirkstall,* an Abbey in times past of no small reckoning, founded by Henry *Lacy,* in the yeere 1147, and at length visiteth *Leedes,* in the Saxon tongue *Loydes,* which became *a house of the kings,* when CAMBODVNVM was by the enemy burnt to the ground: now a rich towne by reason of clothing, where *Oswy* K. of Northumberland put to flight *Penda* the *Mercian: And,* as Bede saith, *this was to the great profit of both nations: for, he both delivered his owne people from the hostile spoiling of the miscreants, and also converted the* Mercians *themselves to the grace of Christian faith.* The very place where in they joyned battaile, the writers call *Winwidfield,* which name I suppose was given it of the victory: like as a place in *Westphalia,* where *Quintilius Varus* with his legions was slaine, is in a Dutch tongue called *Winfield,* that is, *The fields of victory,* as that most learned man and my very good friend Abraham *Ortelius* hath observed. The little region or Territory about it *was* in times past by an old name called *Elmet:* which *Eadwin* King of Northumberland, the sonne of *Aella,* after he had expelled *Cereticus* a British King, conquered in the yeere of Christ 620. Herein is digged limestone everywhere, which is burnt at *Brotherton,* and *Knottingley,* and at certain set times, as it were, at faires, a mighty quantity thereof is conveied to *Wakefield, Sandall,* and *Stanbridge:* and so is sold unto this Western Country which is hilly and somewhat cold, for to manure and enrich their cornefields. But let us leave these things to husbandmen: as for my self I prosesse my ignorance therein, and will goe forward as I beganne.

1612

This survey of the deeds and writings of the manorial tenants was first discovered some time before 1710 in the ruins of Pontefract Castle, then finding its way into a Leeds solicitor's office, and is now in private hands.
Pott, T. 'The Survey of 9 James I (1612)' in *Thoresby Society* LVII (Leeds 1983) pp 72-5.

GENERAL SURVEY

OF THE MANOR OF LEEDS of all and singular lands, tenements, hereditaments, rents, issues and members of the same manor, parcel of the honor of Pontefract, parcel of the jointure of the most excellent lady Anne, Queen of England, Scotland, France and Ireland. Taken at Leeds on

Thursday the 17th day of October in the 9th year of the reign of our lord James, by the grace of god, King of England, France and Ireland, Defender of the Faith etc., and of Scotland the 45th, before THOMAS POTTS, Esq., of Skipwith Woods in the county of York, deputy to THOMAS, LORD KNYVETT, surveyor general of the lands and possession of the same lady, Queen Anne, by virtue of the commission of the said King under the Great Seal of the said Queen directed and handed over to the same Thomas and other commissioners. On the oath of John Falkingham, Esq., of Leeds, in the county of York. Thomas Killingbeck, gent., of the same, John Shann and William Kay, gents. John Cooper, Leonard Stable, Adam Baynes, Christopher Pawson, Robert Harrison, Josiah Jenkinson, John Marshall, William Simpson, Matthew Hudson, William Strickland, William Hargraves, John Fairbarne, Thomas Fountaines, Thomas Hudson, George Greene and Stephen Walker of the same, liveried yeomen and lawful men of the territory and in the neighbourhood of the county of York, who say upon oath that

BUSLINGTHORPE LANE

The circuit of the Manor of Leeds begins at the far end of a certain lane called Leeds Lane leading northwards from the town of Leeds to Chapeltown Moor; and from thence it proceeds as far as a certain lane called Buslingthorpe Lane in the outer part of the same manor, which lane divides the manor of Leeds from the lordship of Scott Hall (parcel), of the lands and possessions of Henry Savile, Knight); and from thence it proceeds northwards from a certain close called Great Mill-Dykes as far as Buslingthorpe; and from thence by a great hill called Lorry Bank, standing within the manor of Leeds.

SHEEPSCAR BECK

There is a certain stream called Sheepscar Beck, flowing by Woodhouse Carr, which, from a certain mill belonging to the said manor of Scott Hall, divides the manor of Leeds from the aforesaid manor of Scott Hall and thence proceeds westwards as far as Pikeman Ridge, dividing the manor of Leeds from the manors of Headingley and Burley, parcels of the lands and possession of John Savile, Knight.

PIKEMAN RIDGE

By the western part of the same . . .called Pikeman Ridge is a certain hedge planted with trees which, on the far side of the aforesaid manor of Leeds, westwards, divides the said lordships of Headingley and Burley from the same manor of Leeds.

ROW OF TREES

Which hedge proceeds southwards from a place called Wreghorne Stile at the far side of a certain common and waste as far as a certain lane exisiting from the King's highway.

GREY STONE, RIVER AIRE

In this lane is an ash-coloured stone (called a Grey Stone) of great size, certainly of great age and antiquity, lying in the middle of the lane, which in the same place divides the manor of Leeds from the aforesaid manors of Headingley and Burley. From the south side of the Grey Stone both the torrent or stream and the aforesaid trees extend circuitously as far as the river Aire, the most celebrated and most excellent river in the northern regions, which river extends by the town of Leeds on the south side of the same.

HIGH-DAM CLOSES

From which river Aire the aforesaid trees extend along towards the east as far as a parcel of land called High-Dam Closes, existing within the manor of Leeds, and a parcel of the land of Robert Portington, Esq. The fence of the closes divides the aforesaid manor of Leeds from the manor of Holbeck, of which manor of Holbeck the most illustrious Prince James, by the grace of God, King of England, Scotland, France and Ireland is the lord.

DRY DITCH

There is a certain lane called Water Lane; from the south side of this lane is a dry ditch leading southwards as far as a close called Bar Croft; and thereafter it extends by the fence of the same close to a stream called Holbeck Beck; and from thence to the south of a certain croft in the tenure of Matthew Hudson; and thereafter it extends on the west of the same croft as far as a lane called Meadow Lane.

MEADOW LANE

From which lane, called Meadow Lane (leading from the town of Beeston as far as the town of Leeds), is a hedge planted with sundry trees which divides the said manor of Leeds from the lands and possessions of John Neville, Knight, now in the tenure of Edward Carey, Knight, southwards on the far side of the same manor as far as the River Aire.

HALL ING, FOSTER CLOSE, LEEDS HOLMES, WOODERSOME DEEP

In the same lane is a small stone bridge below which the stream flows southwards; and thereafter it extends by the fence of a certain close called Hall Ing; and thereafter, circuitously, the fence extends by a certain ditch to the south of an acre of land, lately Thomas Reame's as far as a certain close called Foster Close, parcel of the lands, of the aforesaid Robert Portington, Esq.; and thence it extends eastwards by a certain lane called Hunslet Lane as far as the fence on the east side of a tenement and close in the tenure of Robert Kidd; and thereafter it extends eastwards by a close called Leeds Holmes as far as the river Aire, to a certain place called Woodersome Deep.

STEANDER, PONTEFRACT LANE, NEVILLE HILLS

From this place the boundary of the same manor of Leeds crosses the river Aire and extends on the north side of the same river as far as a parcel of land called the Steander, appurtenant to the vill or small town of Skelton, parcel of the lands and possessions of the duke of Lennox; and thereafter it extends by the fence of the same parcel of land called the Steander as far as a close called the Holt Ing; and thereafter it extends circuitously northwards by a fence and dry ditch as far as a certain lane exisiting from the King's highway leading to the city of York and the borough of Pontefract; by the said lane, fence and dry ditch as far as the south side of a close called the Thorns. On the south side of the same close is a small torrent crossing and extending as far as certain closes called the Neville Hills (formerly lands of the late Thomas Savile Esq.,) and thereafter it extends by a dry ditch northwards to a close (parcel of the Neville Hills) called Orgraves, as far as a certain lane called Leeds Lane, existing from the King's highway from Leeds to the city of York.

LEEDS LANE, WEST BROOME-HILL, GREAT MILL-DYKES

The lane called Leeds Lane extends southwards to the east side of a close called West Broome-Hill; and thereafter it

extends circuitously northwards by a certain close; and thereafter the fence of the same close called West Broome-Hill is the boundary of the same manor, extending westwards as far as a certain lane leading from Leeds to Coldcotes; and thence it leads, by the same lane, between the lands

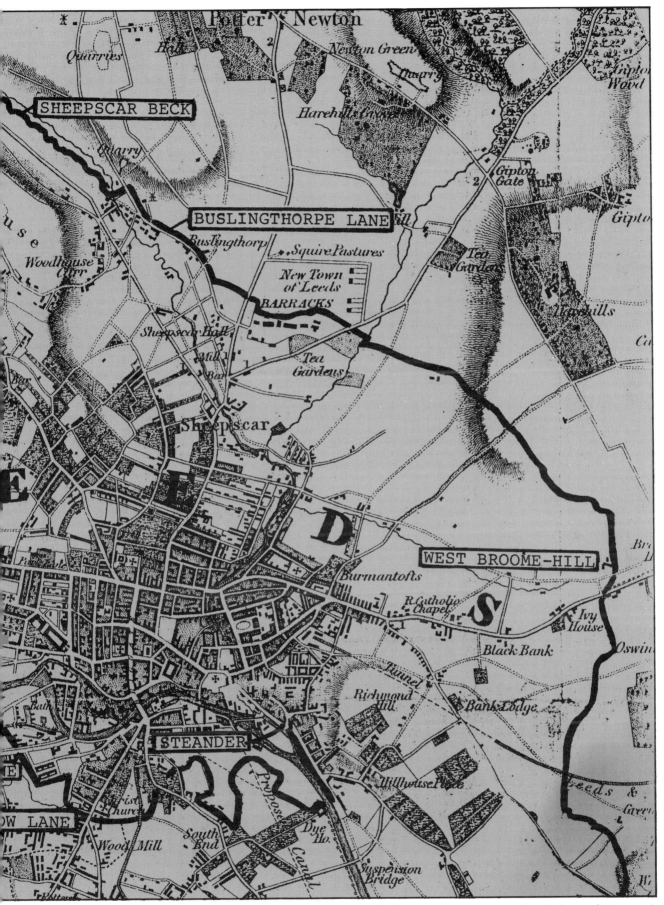

The boundaries of the Manor of Leeds, as described in the Survey of 1612. Here they are superimposed on Baines and Newsome's Map of the Borough of Leeds of 1834.

pertaining to the lordship of Potternewton on the north side, and John Falkingham's lands on the south side as far as the stream or torrent issuing from Gipton or 'Gledell Well'; and thence westwards by the same stream to a close called Little Mill-Dykes, and it extends by the lane called Leeds Lane as far as the aforesaid close called Great Mill-Dykes.

Thus he defines the circuit of the manor of Leeds.

Which noteworthy or special aforesaid places named Buslingthorpe Lane, Sheepscar Beck, Pikeman Ridge, Hedge planted with trees (called Row of Trees), the hugh ash-coloured stone (called Grey-Stone) the river Aire, High-Dam Closes, the dry ditch (called the Dry Ditch), the lane called Meadow Lane, Hall Ing, Foster Close, Leeds Holmes, Woodersome Deep, Steander, Pontefract Lane, Neville Hills, Leeds Land, West Broome-Hill and Great Mill-Dykes are and always of old have been the limits or particular bounds, marks and boundaries of the whole of the precinct or circuit of the aforesaid manor of Leeds.

Examined by Thomas Potts.

1626

On 13 July 1626, King Charles I granted a Charter of Incorporation which established Leeds as a Borough, governed by an Alderman and Burgesses. The following is a translation of the Latin text of the original charter.

Wardell, J. *Municipal History of the Borough of Leeds* (Leeds 1846) XXXI-XXXII.

Charter of Incorporation of the Borough of Leeds (Translation) 2nd Charles I., 13 July 1626.

The King to all to whom these present shall come, greeting. Whereas our town of Leeds in our county of York, is an ancient and populous town, and the inhabitants of the town and parish of Leeds aforesaid, for many years past, have had, and skilfully exercised in the said town and parish, the art of mystery of making and working woollen cloths, commonly called in English 'northern dozens', to their perpetual praise, and great increase of the revenue of the crown of England for the custom of the same cloths. And whereas we are informed by the humble petition of our beloved subjects, the clothiers and inhabitants of the said town and parish of Leedes, that the cloths heretofore made in the said town and parish, have been sold and exported before other cloths of the country there, from their fit, good, and true workmanship, and make, and that from the fame and estimation of the same cloths, divers, clothiers of the same town and parish had begun to make, and as yet endeavour to make deceptive cloths, and to dye the same with wood called logwood, to the damage and prejudice of us, subversion of the clothiers of the town and parish aforesaid, the discredit of the inhabitants there, if immediate remedy for that purpose be not applied, and that divers other enormities and inconveniences for some time have sprung up, and do still increase, as well concerning the cloths aforesaid, as the town and parish aforesaid, which in no way can be reformed without good rule, by our royal authority and power, be established. AND THEREUPON they most humbly have besought us, so far as we are able, and inasmuch as we may be willing in this behalf, most graciously to extend our royal favour and munificence to the same inhabitants, and that we would vouchsafe by our letters patent, to make, constitute, and create, for the most honourable and better rule and government and improvement of the town and parish aforesaid, the said inhabitants into a body corporate and politic, and also the town aforesaid into a borough, with a grant of certain liberties, privileges, immunities, and franchises, as to us better should seem fit to be made. WE CONSIDERING the premises, and willing that henceforth for ever there should continually be had, one certain and undoubted manner, as well for direction of the artificers, us for keeping the peace, good rule, and government of our people there, and that our peace be kept, and acts of justice

there be done, without further delay; and hoping that if the inhabitants of the town and parish aforesaid, should enjoy by our grant, more ample honours, liberties, and privileges, that then they will feel themselves more especially and stronger bound to perform services which it may be in their power to bestow upon us our heirs and successors. Of our special grace, and of our certain knowledge and mere motion, we have willed, ordained, granted and appointed, and by these presents, for us our heirs and successors, do will, ordain, grant, and appoint, that the aforesaid town of Leedes, in the aforesaid county of York, shall from henceforth for ever, be and remain a free Borough of itself; and that the said borough of Leedes, and the circuit jurisdiction and precinct thereof, from henceforth for ever shall extend and spread themselves, and shall and may be able to extend and reach into and through the whole town and parish of Leedes aforesaid. AND that all houses, buildings, lands, waters, water-courses, soil and ground, situate, lying, and being within the town and parish of Leedes aforesaid, from henceforth for ever, may and shall be within the limits, metes, bounds, and juridiction of the said borough of Leedes, and for ever shall be called and known by the name of the BOROUGH OF LEEDES in THE COUNTY OF YORK. AND that all and singular the inhabitants of the aforesaid town and parish of Leedes, and their successors, from henceforth for ever may, and shall be a body corporate and politic, in matter, fact, and name, by the name of the ALDERMAN AND BURGESSES OF THE BOROUGH OF LEEDS IN THE COUNTY OF YORK.

1628

This description was prepared by Nicholas Raynton and Arnold Child, representatives of the City of London. It is one of the first to give an account of the physical appearance of the town. At this time Briggate was mainly lined with ancient, mean and low-built half-timbered houses 'straightened on theire back-sides'.

'The Mannor of LEEDES called the Mayne Rydinge' (in 1628). Quoted in Beresford, M.W. *Time & Place; Collected Essays* (1984) pp.302-3.

LEEDES is an Ancient Markett Towne some 10 or 12 miles Northwest beyond Pontefract, and 6 miles Northward beyond Wakefield, (another great Markett Towne). It standeth pleasantlie in a fruitefull and enclosed vale; upon the North side of the same River of Eyre, over or beyond a stone bridge, from whence it hath a large and broad streete (paved with stone) leadinge directlie North and continuallie ascendinge. The houses on both sides thereof are verie thicke, and close compacted together, beinge ancient meane and lowe built; and generallie all of Tymber; though they have stone quarries frequent in the Towne, and about it; only some fewe of the richer sort of the Inhabitants have theire houses more large and capacious: yett all lowe and straightened on theire back-sides. In the middle of the streete (towards the upper end wheare the Markett place standeth) is built the Court or Moote House (as they terme it) and from thence upward are the shambles, with a narrow streete on both sides, much annoyinge the whole Town; yett for theire Conveniencie, and wante of roome, not to be avoided, or placed elsewhere. The Kinges Mannor (now the Cities) is called the Mayne ridinge lyinge rounde about the Towne of Leeds; scarce anie waie a mile from it, some parte of it streacheth over the river of Ayre, lyinge on the South side of the stone bridge, conteynine about 20 or 30 acres on which is built soe manie or more houses, now copiholds divided all into small parcells, and excellent ground, meadowe and pasture. George Shires hath about 3 acres thereof on which is newly built a faire house paying 4s per Annum rent. It is conceived this is parte of the Demesnes call the Hall Ings as the verie name still Imports. Robert Sowden houldeth another parte therof with a house alsoe, purchased of Mr Samuell Casson late Alderman of Leeds.

THIS Mannor is all enclosed and lieth in verie small parcells as some halfe an acre, some 2 acres some more, manie lesse haveinge houses scattered frequentlie and throughout the whole lordshipp, by reason of theire great Clothinge on which trade the whole Towne, cheefely, and in a maner wholie dependeth.

The parish of Leedes stretcheth itselfe farr beyond the Mannor every waie invirroninge the same rounde about, and conteyninge therin six free chappells and soe manie preachinge ministers, and yett the Church of Leeds (which is a verie faire church built after a Cathedrall structure and having one side thereof double Iled) is soe besett with scaffold over scaffold, so as noe place is voide to heare ye Minister. *6. free chappells in Leeds parish.*

The ground in this Mannor is all generallie good and certainly in that place cannot be lesse worth than 4 nobles and 30s an acre and I am verily persuaded they are lett at a dearer rate; Though we could learne little of the tenants, who generallie as it were in a subtle combination, mixt with feare would have concealed, and obscured even palpable thinges.

Upper Woodhouse and Nether Woodhouse are parcell of this Mannor and lye Northwest from the Towne of Leeds some parte close adjoininge. *Woodhouse a member of Leeds.*

Knowsthropp (or rather Knaves-Thorpe) lyeth about a myle East from the Towne and is the more fruitefull place, where dewelleth but 4 coppi-houlders houldinge about 80 acres apeece.

Theire names are
1. Richard Sikes a burger of Leeds.
2. Adam Baynes
3. John Cowper
4. William Stable
4 tenants of Knvesthorpe a member of Leeds.

These have onlie a common pasture betweene themselves lyinge beneath Knowsthorp upon the River Eyre; very rich ground conteyninge about 16 or 20 acres (as we conceived) and over the river on the south side of this common where the forde goeth over, lyeth the stayner (but in Rothwell parish) a peece of pasture in Common to them alsoe and conteyninge about 7 acres for which they paie yearly to the Kinte 9s they have a late coppie of it made by one Tusser as we were Informed. *Knowstrop Common. The stayner in Rothwell parish.*

The other common and wast belonginge to this Mannor are called Woodhouse Moore conteyninge as we conceive about 50 or 60 acres this is light grounde and lyinge upon a high hill haveinge manie small cottages rounde about and adjoininge upon it. In this Common hath beene a Cole myne, now not used; yett in lease with these mynes of Knowsthrop payinge for this 20s per annum ut infra. *Common called Woodhouse Moore 50 or 60 acres. Colemyne not used in lease with others of Knowstrop.*

1631

IN 1631 the plague was ravaging West Yorkshire, threatening both personal life and the economic prosperity of the region. In this letter,

written from York on 22 September 1631, Lord Wentworth informs the government of his fears.
Cartwirght, J. *Chapters in the history of Yorkshire (1872) p.243-4 The letter was written at York on 22 September 1631.*

LORD WENTWORTH TO VISCOUNT DORCHESTER.

"My very good Lord,

"It is full time in my judgement to give your Lo a shortt accompt of our presentt condition in thes parttes, wch as it shall seeme good in your better wisedom, may be made knowen to his Maty., or my Lords of the Counsell in case you would dirette us, any thing more to be dun then is allready.

"True itt is (that leaving our neigboures of Lancishire and Lincolnshire miserably distressed with the pestilence) that now within thes sixe weeks, the infection is cunnd to our selves in divers partts of this County, and last of all into this Citty. Upon the edge of Lancishire, ther is the toune of Heptonstall, wch hath meare forty howses infected; Mirfeild a little toune not farre of itt, hath lost ninoscore persons, and both these tounes wthn four miles of Hallifax, wch yet God be praysed, stands sownde, but much indangered, by reason of the great number of people, and lardge wade of clothing theraboutes. It is likewise in the tow tounes of Beeston and Holbecke, wch are wthn one mile of Leedes, and if it should please God to visit either of thos greate tounes, Hallifax or Leedes, wch tow allone trade more then all the country besides, in good faithe it would mightily distresse and impoverishe all that side of the Cuntrye.

1643

Leeds was occupied successively by the opposing factions in the English Civil War, but the most heated action took place on 23 January 1643, when it was captured by General Sir Thomas Fairfax, the great Parliamentary commander. This description is his personal account of the battle.
Fairfax, T. *The Memoirs of General Fairfax . . .(1776) pp.32-7*

On Monday, being the 23 of January 1643, I marched from Bradford with six troops of horse and three companies of dragoons, under the command of Sir Henry Fowles, my Comissary, or Lieutenant General of horse; and near 1000 musketeers and 2000 club-men, under the command of Sir William Fairfax, Colonel and Lieutenant General of the foot, one company of these also being dragoons, under Capt. Mildmay; about 30 musketeers and 1000 club-men marked on the south-side toward Wakefield, the rest on the north-side toward Woodhouse moor. On the west-side we commended the cause to God by prayer: I dispatched a trumpeter to Sir William Saville, commander in Chief at Leeds, under the Earl of Newcastle, requiring, in writing, the town to be delivered to me for the King and Parliament, to which Sir William desdainfully answered immediately, and said, he used not to give answer to such frivolous demands, and that he wondered Sir Thomas would be so uncivil as to come so near the town before he had acquainted him with it; and that there might be more virtue in his actions than in that paper sent him: So confident he seemed to be, with the strength he had in the Town, he could well enough keep it, wherein were about 2000 men, namely 1500 foot and 500 troops of horse and dragoons, and two pieces of cannon. This summons, being thus refused, we approached nearer the south-west-side of the town with our forces, and being within view there-of, with our banners displayed, (being about 36 colours) I sent another trumpeter to Sir William Saville, who shortly after, by a trumpeter, assured

General Sir Thomas Fairfax of Denton Park near Otley (1611-1671), whose diary of 23 Janury 1643 recorded his capture of Leeds for Parliament during the English Civil Wars.

us that we should get nothing but by fight, whereupon we prepared for an assualt, and instantly drew out of our companies five colours of our most expert soldiers, and appointed them to march down with Captain Forbes, Captain Briggs, Lee, Frank and Palmer, with his dragoons on foot, toward the water along the trenches, near to, and above which about 100 musketeers were drawn out of the town on a hill, and about one o'clock in the afternoon, they gave fire from the inside of their works upon our musketeers, who approaching nearer, shrouded themselves under a hill and let fly at the said centry, with no loss at all on either side, they within the trenches shooting too high, and the other at the trenches, and thus the fight began between them most

fiercely: Now we having the work, which was, *Emanuel*, and every commander in their several stations, gave charges and commands and riding from place to place encouraged their men to fall on resolutely; who being mightily emboldened by their valient leaders, performed the same with admirable courage; and although most of them were but unexperienced fresh-water men, taken up about Bradford and Halifax, but upon the Saturday before, yet they came up on most resolutely and valiantly, especially the musketeers under Sir William Fairfax, Commander of the foot, who most courageously, at the head of his regiment, and in the face of the enemy stormed the town most furiously, whereupon began very hot service; Captain Forbes also behaving himself most vallantly about the enemy's trenches and out-works, from whence they played very sharply against our men, but were as hotly answered by us with admirable courage and fearless resolution, under the conduct of this nobel Captian; insomuch that notwithstanding the enemy's utmost endeavours to oppose us, together with the assistance of their cannon which were often discharged upon our men, yet they soon killed their cannoniers, and after a furious fight of two hours, our men most bravely beat them quite from their works, when bullets flew about, our men's ears as thick as hail, yet myself, Sir William Fairfax, and Sir Henry Fowles on one side, and the resolute Captain Forbes with his brace company on the other side, made way into the town most furiously sword in hand, and violent force of arms, being closely followed by the dauntless club-men, and so with much difficulty got possession thereof within the space of two hours, wherin were found two brass cannon and good store of arms and ammunition, which we presently seized; we took also four colours, and 500 prisoners among whom were six commanders, most of the rest were common soldiers, who upon taking an oath never to fight in this cause, against the King and Parliament, were set at liberty and suffered to depart, but unarmed. There were not above forty slain, whereof ten or twelve at the most on our side, the rest on theirs; Serjeant Major Beaumont, in his flight, endeavouring to cross the river to save his life, lost it by being drowned therein; and Sir William Saville, their General, in his flight also crossing the same river hardly escaped the same fate. Thus, by the Lord's mighty and most merciful assistance, we obtained a great and glorious victory, which may so appear considering the town was so strongly fortified with out-works, and so well manned within, as was before mentioned; which also did strike such terror into the Earl of Newcastle's army, that the several garrisons of Wakefield, Sherbourn, and Pontefract, fled all away presently before any assualted them, some few only excepted that stayed at Pontefract castle to keep it.

The consequence of this action was yet of more importance; for those who fled from Leeds to Wakefield, and quitting that Garrison also, gave my Lord of Newcastle such an alarm at Pontefract, that he drew all his army again to York, leaving once more a free intercourse, which he had so long time cut off, betwixt my father and us.

1664

Marmaduke Rawdon (1610-69) of York spent most of his adult life in overseas trade, after which he travelled extensively in England, recording his experiences in a journal, which unfortunately does not survive. This account comes from an anonymous biography taken from the journal before its disappearance.
'The life of Marmaduke Rawdon of York' *Camden Society*, 85 (1863) pp.120-121 *The Year referred to is 1664.*

From thence they went to Leedes, a rich towne of clothinge, where are many very rich men; here one Mr John Harison, a clothier, built one parish church, a very faire one, of free stone, and a faire steple with four bells; itt haith in itt six rankes of paewes of exelent wrought wainscott, the roffe of the church all freet worke. He founded an hospital of twentie almes howses; he built likewisse a chapell to itt, and a howse for a vicar to live and say prayers to them he built a free schoole all of free stone; he built a wholle street with faire howses on booth sides, the howse next the church beinge for the parson of the parish; and att his owne proper cost

and charge did all this, and left large revenews to maintaine thesse thinges, which were all finisht about 30 years agoe.

Thursday, the 4 August, they went from hence to Kirstall Abbey, tow miles from Rawdon, a towne where the fameley of the Rawdons haith continued ever sence the Conquest, and in this monastery had thir place of buriall, and were to itt greate benefactors; a stately abey itt was, and some part of itt yett standinge.

1673

Richard Blome (d.1705) compiled and published many reference books describing Carolean England.
Blome, R. *Britannia* (1673) p.258.

Leeds, scuituate on the *Ayr*, an ancient *Town*, where formerly the *Kings* had their *Royal Palace;* and here *Oswy* King of the *Northumbers* put to flight *Penda* the *Mercian*. It is at present a large and well-built *Town-Corporate* governed by a *Maior* and *Aldermen*, with other *Sub-Officers*, electeth *parliament men*, is very well inhabited, especially by wealthy *Clothiers*, who drive a great *trade* for their *cloth;* and hath two considerable *Markets* on *Tuesdays* and *Saturdays*, which are well *traded* unto for *corn, provisions, woollen-cloth*, and divers good *commodities*.

1688

In December 1688, Leeds was alarmed by reports that the retreating Irish army of the former King James II was about to attack the town. Ralph Thoresby provided the following description of this exciting event.
Atkins, D.H. *Ralph Thoresby the topographer: his Town and Times* (1885) pp.263-265.

"Only I cannot omit the dreadful alarm of the flying army of Irish, and massacring Papists, who with unheard of cruelty burnt and killed all before them. Watch and ward were kept every night by the principal inhabitants of Leeds in their own persons, and despatches sent to bring intelligence, so that on Monday there were assembled at Leeds, about seven thousand horse and foot, in defence of their lives and liberties, religion and property, against those barbarous and inhuman wretches.

"These were digested into several troops and companies, under Sir John Kay, colonel; Sir William Wentworth, lieutenant, colonel: Mr Nevile of Chevet, major; it would be endless to enter into detail of the captains and subalterns. Our fears were now somewhat abated, when all upon the sudden at night they were raised to the height upon a most dreadful alarm, 'Horse and arms, horse and arms! the enemy are upon us — Beeston is actually burnt, and only some escaped to bring the doleful tidings! The drums beat, the bells rang backward, the women shrieked, and such dreadful consternation seized upon all persons; some men with their wives and children left all behind them (even monies and plate upon the tables) and ran for shelter to the barns and haystacks in the fields.

"Their horrow was so great and universal that the aged people who remembered the Civil Wars said they never knew anything like it.

Thousands of lighted candles were placed in the windows, and persons of any courage and consideration (if such a thing was to be found) ran with their arms to the Bridge, and so marched towards Beeston; so that in a very small time some thousands appeared, and I among the rest, with horse and arms; and, blessed be God! the terror disappeared, it being a false alarm, taken from some drunken people, who cried out horribly, Murder! Murder!

I had left a cabinet with some of the most valuable moveables for my dear to cast into the well; but she had that presence of mind, after I was mounted and gone, to go up to the turret, and told the females Beeston was safe; for if but one house was on fire, it might be discovered there.

The town being pretty well satisfied, were generally gone to bed; but about midnight was a more dreadful alarm than the former a knocking at every door, 'Fire! Fire!' 'Horse and Arms! for God's sake!' It was a piteous sight to observe the terror and confusion that all sorts of persons were now in. I was most concerned for my dear wife, who was in the family way; and when I was mounted again, I could see nothing but paleness and horror in the countenances of all men. Our scouts had brought word that Halifax beacon was burning as a general warning to the country, and that Halifax and Huddersfield were burnt. The first part was really true, though from a mistaken panic and fear that had seized them as well as us.

But no enemy appearing near, and watch being set at several passes, I lay me down again, but with my clothes on; and when I awoke, rejoiced to see the light of another day, when my Lord Fairfax came to town with three or four troops of horse, completely armed, and we slept more securely, the expresses bringing pretended advice that the Irish had broke into parties and dispersed.

Upon the whole, this matter of the alarm, which was general, and spread over most parts of England, was managed so artfully, that even when all was over, I could never learn who was concerned, even in this neighbourhood."

1698

Celia Fiennes (1662-1741) travelled on horseback throughout England in the reign of William III, carefully noting her detailed observations and opinions of everything she saw. Her manuscripts were not written for publication, and remained unprinted for two hundred years.
The Journal of Celia Fiennes written in 1698.

Leeds is a large town, severall large streetes cleane and well pitch'd and good houses all built of stone, some have good gardens and steps up to their houses and walls before them; this is esteemed the wealthyest town of its bigness in the country, its manufacture is the woollen cloth the Yorkshire Cloth in which they are all employ'd and are esteemed very rich and very proud; they have provision soe plentifull that they may live with very little expense and get much variety; here if one calls for a tankard of ale which is allwayes a groate-its the only dear thing all over Yorkshire, their ale is very strong-but for paying this groat for your ale you may

have a slice of meate either hott or cold according to the tyme of day you call, or else butter and cheese gratis into the bargaine, this was a generall custom in most parts of Yorkshire but now they have almost changed it, and tho' they still retaine the great price for the ale yet make Strangers pay for their meate, and at some places at great rates, notwithstanding how cheape they have all their provision; there is still this custome on a Market day at Leeds the sign of the Bush just by the bridge, any body that will goe and call for one tanckard of ale and a pinte of wine and pay for these only, shall be set to a table to eate with 2 or 3 dishes of good meate and a dish of sweetmeates after; had I known this and the day which was their market, I would have come then but I happened to come a day after the Market, however I did only pay for 3 tankards of ale and what I eate and my servants was gratis; this town is full of Discenters there are 2 large Meeting places, here is also a good schoole for young Gentlewomen; the streetes are very broad the Market large.

1715

Ralph Thoresby (1658-1715) followed his father's profession as a cloth-merchant, but his main interests lay in the fields of history and anitquities. His monumental *Ducatus Leodiensis* of 1715 is the first published history of Leeds, and also one of the first generation of English parish histories. Today his work is still a major source of information for the study of the history of the town.
Thoresby, R. *Ducatus Leodiensis or the Topography of the Town and Parish of Leedes* (1715) pp.1 & 14.

The greatest part of this ancient and populous Town stands upon the North Side of the River *Are,* upon an easy Ascent; the Topographical Description of which is begun at the West Part, because there of old stood a famous Castle with a Park adjoining, which, though now converted into lesser Inclosures, yet remains the Name of the *Park* to this Day, and gives Denomination also to the Lane on the North Side thereof.

This Castle was beseiged by King *Stephen* in his March towards *Scotland, Anno* 1139; and here was the unfortunate Prince, King *Richard* II. lodged some time befoe his barbarous Murder in *Pontefract, Castle;* but these matters are to be more fully discussed in the Historical Part. Out of the Park issued a Yearly Rent of Eight Pounds to the Crown, which with others arising from the Mills, & c, are now the Property of his Grace the High Puissant and most Nobel Prince, *Thomas Osborne,* Duke of *Leedes,* Marquis of *Camarthen,* Earl of *Danby,* Viscount *Latimer,* Baron *Osborn* of *Kiveton* (vulgo *Keeton)* and Baronet; Lord President of his Majesty's most Honourable Privy-Council, Lord Leiutenant of the East, West, and North-Ridings in the County of *York,* of the City

This prospect of Leeds in 1712 by William Lodge, shows the town from Water Lane, on the south bank of the River Aire. Note the man fishing in the Hol beck to the left, and the long pieces of cloth drying and stretching on the tenters on Tenter Lane, in the centre of the view. It gives a splendid impression of the size and character of the town recorded in the travelogue of Celia Fiennes.

of *York,* and County of the same; as also *Custos Rotulorum* for the East-Riding of *Yorkshire,* and the Liberties of *Ripon* and *Cawood* in the said County, Governour of his Majesty's Town and Fortress of *Kingston* upon *Hull,* and Knight of the most noble Order of the Garter . . .

In this spacious Street, which from the *Bridge* at the Foot of it, is called *Bridge-Gate,* or, in our Northern Dialect, which retains much of the *Saxon, Brig-gate, bricz vel briz pons,* stood many of the ancient *Borough-Houses,* which to this Day pay a certain *Burgage-Rent* to the Lords of the Mannor of *Leedes.* The famour *Cloth-Market,* the Life not of the Town alone, but these Parts of *England,* is held in this street, *sub dio,* twice every Week, *viz* upon *Tuesdays* and *Saturdays,* early in the Mornings. The Brig End shots have made as great a Noise amongst the Vulgar, where the Clothier may, together with his Pot of Ale, have a Noggin O'Porage, and a Trencher of either Boil'd or Roast-Meat for Two-pence, as the Market itself, amongst the more Judicious, where several thousand Pounds worth of Broad-Cloth are bought, and, generally speaking, paid for (except the Water-Lengths, which cannot then be determined) in a few Hours Time, and this with so profound a silence as is surprizing to Strangers, who from the adjoining Galleries, & c, can hear no more Noise than the lowly Murmur of the Merchant upon the *Exchange at London.* After the signal is given by the Bell at the old Chapel by the Bridge, the Cloth and Benches are removed, so that the Street is at Liberty for the Market People of other Provessions, as the Country Linen-Drapers, Shoo-makers, Hard-ware-Men, and the Sellers of Wood-Vessels, Wicker-Baskets, Wanded-Chairs, Flats & c. Fruit of all sorts are brought in so vast Quantities, that *Halifax,* and other considerable Markets, are frequently supplied from hence, the Mayor's Officers have number'd five hundred Loads of Apples only, upon one Day. Above the Market for the Milk-Cows, is the *Ichthyopolium,* which, notwithstanding its great Distance from the Sea, is weekly twice or thrise, if not oftner, plentifully furnished with great Variety of Fish, though short, I confess, of *Preston* in *Amounderness,* where the Fish-Toll, at 1d a Horse Load, and 4d, a Cart, has sometimes amounted to six Shillings a Day, as I am informed by a neighbouring Justice of the Peace. A little above this is the *Moot-Hall* in the Front of the *Middle-Row,* on one side of which is one of the best furnished *Flesh-Shambles* in the north of *England;* on the other, the *Wool-market* for *Broad-Cloth,* which is the All in All. From the *Cross,* which is well stock'd with Poultry, and other proper Appurtenances, to the *New Street,* is the *Corn-Market,* which is very considerable; and the more so, because the Populousness of the Places makes it yield greater Profit to the Husband-men than other Markets do. In the *Upper-Head-Row* is the *Horse-Fair,* and in the *Lower,* the *Forum Swuarium;* and in other parts of the Town, whatever is necesary for comfortable Sustenance of Mankind, though too tedious particularly to recite.

*c.*1720

Daniel Defoe (*c.*1661-1731) was a novelist, journalist, and political spy. Although his *Tour* was first published in the mid 1720s, he had been making notes for it for over thirty years, and so his description cannot be closely dated.
Defoe, D. *A tour thro' the whole Island of Great Britain, divided into circuits or journeys (1724-7).*

Leeds is a large, wealthy and populous Town, it stands on the North Bank of the Rivers Aire, or rather on both sides the river, for there is a large suburb or Part of the Town on the South Side of the River, and the whole is joined by a stately and prodigiously strong Stone Bridge, so large, and so wide, that formerly the Cloth market was kept in neither Part of the Town, but on the very Bridge itself; and therefore the Refreshment given the Clothiers by the Inn-Keepers, of which I shall speak presently, is called the Brigg-shot of this day.

The Encrease of the Manufacturers and the Trade, soon made the Market too great to be confined to the Brigg or Bridge, and it is now kept in the High-Street, beginning from the Bridge, and running up North almost to the Market-House, where the ordinary market for Provisions begins, which also is the greatest of its kind in all the North of England, except Halifax, of which I have spoken already, nay the People of Leeds will not allow me to except Halifax, but say, that theirs is the greatest Market, and that not the greatest Plenty only, but the best of all Kinds of Provisions are brought hither.

But this is not the Case; it is the Cloth Market I am now to describe, which is indeed a Prodigy of its kind, and is not to be equalled in the world. The Market for Serges at Exeter is indeed a wonderful thing, and the value sold here

Francis Place's 'Prospect of Leeds from the Knostrop Road' shows the town from the east. On the left, a sailing barge approaches Leeds Lock, part of the Aire and Calder Navigation's recent improvement which enabled vessels to approach the Town Warehouse near Leeds Bridge. This was one of the illustrations published in Ralph Thoresby's Ducatus Leodiensis *of 1715.*

is very great; but then the Market there is but once a Week, here it is twice a week, and the quantity of goods vastly great too.

The Market itself is worth describing, thou' no Description can come up to the Thing itself; however, take a Sketch of it with its Customs and Usages as follows:

The street is a large, broad, fair and well-built Street, beginning, as I have said, at the Bridge, and ascending gently to the North.

Early in the morning, there are Tressels placed in two Rows in the Street, sometimes two Rows on a side, but always one Row at least, then there are Boards laid cross those Tressles, so that the Boards lie like long Counters on either side, from one end of the Street to the other.

The Clothiers come early in the morning with their Cloth; and as few Clothiers bring more than one Piece, the Market being so frequent, they go into the Inns and Publick-Houses with it, and there set it down.

At seven a clock in the morning, the Clothiers being supposed to be all come by that time, even in the winter, but the House is varied as the seasons advance (in the summer earlier, in the depth of winter a little later) I take it, as a medium, and as it was when I was there, at six or seven, I say, the Market Bell rings; it would surprise a Stranger to see in how few Minutes, without hurry or noise, and not

the least disorder, the whole Market is fill'd; all the Boards upon the Tressells are covered with Cloth, close to one another as the Pieces can lie long ways by one another, and behind every Piece of Cloth, the Clothier standing to sell it.

This indeed is not so difficult, when we consider that the whole quentity is brought into the Market as soon as one Piece, because as the Clothiers stand ready in the Inns and Shops just behind, and that there is a Clothier to every Piece, they have no moe to do, but, like a Regiment drawn up in line, every one takes up his Piece, and has about five Steps to march to lay it upon the first Row of Boards, and perhaps ten to the second row; so that upon the Market Bell ringing, in half a quarter of an House the whole Market is fill'd, the Rows of Boards cover'd, and the Clothiers stand ready.

As soon as the Bell has done Ringing, the Merchants and Factors, and Buyers of all sorts, come down, and coming along the Spaces between the Rows of Boards, they walk up the Rows, and down as their occasions direct. Some of them have their foreign Letters of Orders, with Patterns seal'd on them, in Rows, in their Hands; and with those they match Colours, holding them to the Cloths as they think they agree to: when they see any Cloths to their colours, or that suit their occasions, they reach over to the Clothier and whisper, and in the fewest words imaginable the Price is stated; one asks, the other bids; and 'its agree, or not agree, in a Moment.

The merchants and buyers generally walk down and up twice on each side of the rows, and in little more than an houre all the business is done; in less than half an hour you will percieve the cloths begin to move off, the Clothier taking it up upon his shoulder to carry it to the merchant's House; and by half an hour after eight a clock the market Bell rings again; immediately the Buyers disappear, the Cloth is all sold, or if here and there a Piece happens not to be bought, 'tis carried back into the Inn, and, in a quarter of an House, there is not a Piece of Cloth to be seen in the Market.

Thus, you see, Ten or Twenty thousand Pounds value in Cloth, and sometimes much more, bought and sold in little more than an hour, and the laws of the market the most strictly observed as ever I saw done in any market in England; for

1. Before the market Bell rings again, no man shews a piece of cloth, nor can the Clothiers sell any but in open market.

2. After the Market Bell rings again, no body stays a moment in the market, but carries his cloth back if it be not sold.

3. And that which is most admirable is, 'tis all managed with the most profound silence, and you cannot hear a Word spoken on the whole market, I mean, by the persons buying and selling, 'tis all done in whisper.

The reason of this silence, is cheifly because the Clothiers stand so near to one another; and 'tis always reasonable that one should not know what another does, for that would be discovering their business, and exposing it to one another.

If a Merchant has bidden a Clothier a Price, and he will not take it, he may go after him to his house, and tell him he has considered of it, and is willing to let him have it: but they are not to make any new Agreement for it, so as to remove the Market from the Street to the Merchant's House.

By nine a clock the Boards are taken down, the Tressels are removed, and the Street cleared, so that you see no market or goods any more than if there had been nothing to do; and this is done twice a week. By this quick return the clothiers are constantly supplied with money, their workmen are duly paid, and a prodigious sum circulates thro' the county every week.

If you should ask upon all this, where all these Goods,

Around 1726 John Cossins produced the first published map of Leeds. His 'New & Exact Plan' features illustrations of all the town's major buildings and merchant's mansions, including the newly-built Trinity Church on Boar Lane. Serving the wealthy merchant community, William Etty's design had the Golden Fleece on the weather-vane, and also on the lead fall-pipes.

as well here as at Wakefield, and at Hallifax, are vented and disposed of? It would require a long Treatise of Commerce to enter into that Part: But that I may not bring you into the Labyrinth, and not show you the way out, I shall, in three short Heads, describe the consumption, for there are three channels by which it goes:

1. For the home Consumption; their goods being, as I may say, every where made us of, for the cloathing the ordinary people, who cannot go to the Price of the fine Medley Cloths made, as I formerly gave you an account, in the Western Counties of England. There are for this purpose a set of travelling Merchants in Leeds, who go all over England with Droves of Pack Horses, and to all the Fairs and Market Towns over the whole island, I think I may say none excepted. Here they supply not the common people by retail, which would denominate them Pedlars indeed, but they supply the shops by wholesale or whole pieces; and not only so, but give large credit too, so that they are really travelling merchants, and as such they sell a very great Quantity of goods; 'tis ordinary for one of these men to carry a thousand pounds value of cloth with them at a time, and having sold it at the Fairs or Towns where they go, they send their horses back for as much more, and this very often in a summer, for they chose to travel in the summer, and perhaps towards the winter time, tho' as little in Winter as they can, because of the badness of the Roads.

2. Another sort of buyers are those who buy to send to London; either by Commissions from London, or they give Commissions to Factors and Warehouse-keepers in London to sell for them; and these drive also a very great Trade: These Factors and Warehouse-keepers not only supply all the shop keepers and wholesale Men in London, but sell also very great Quantities to the merchants, as well for Exportation to the English Colonies in America, which take off great quantities of those course goods, especially New England, New York, Virginia, & c. as also to the Russia Merchants, who send an exceeding quantity to Peterborough, Riga, Dantzic, Narva, and to Sweden and Pomerania.

3. The third sort of buyers, and who are not less considerable than the other, are truly merchants, that is to say, such as receive commissions from abroad to buy cloth for the merchants chiefly in Hamburgh, and in Holland, and from several other parts; and these are not only many in Number, but some of them are very considerable in their Dealings, and correspond as far as Nuremberg, Frankfort, Leipsick, and even to Vienna and Ausburgh, in the farthest Provinces of Germany.

On account of this trade it was, that some years ago an Act of Parliament was obtained for making the rivers Aire and Calder Navigable; by which a communication by Water was opened from Leeds and Wakefield to Hull, and by which means all the woollem manufactures which those merchants now export by commission, as above, is carried by water to Hull and there shipped for Holland, Bremen, Hamburgh, and the Baltick. And thus you hae a brief account, by what methods this cast manufacture is carried off, and which way they find a vent for it.

There is another trade in this Part of the country, which

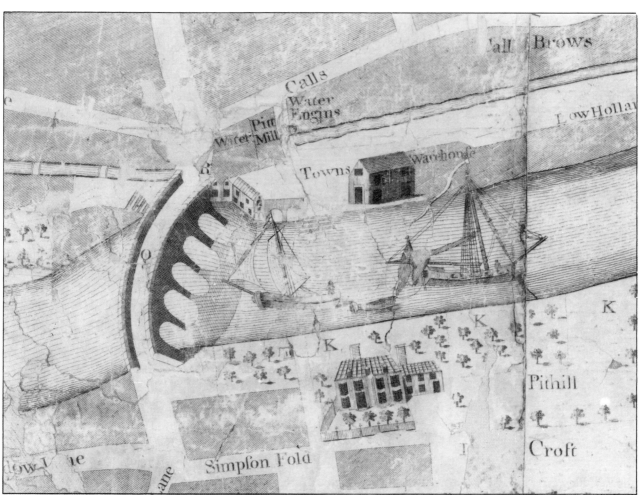

The Navigation enabled goods to be transported by water to and from North Sea ports up to Leeds Bridge. This detail of Cossin's plan shows the bridge, with its steps made from the ruins of Kirkstall Abbey, the water engine installed by George Sorocold in 1695 to provide a water supply for the town, and the Town Warehouse, where goods were stored for collection and despatch.

is now become very considerable since the opening the navigation to these rivers, and that is, that from hence they carry coals down from Wakefield (especially) and also from Leeds, at both which they have a very great quantity, and such, as they told me, could never be exhausted. These they carry quite down into the Humber, and then up to the Ouse to York, and up the Trent, and other rivers, where there are abundance of large towns, who they supply with coals; with this advantage too, that whereas the Newcastle coals pay four shillings per Chaldron Duty to the publick; these being only called River Borne Coal, are exempted, and pay nothing; though, strictly speaking, they are carried on the Sea too, for the Humber is properly the Sea. But they have been hitherto exempted from the Tax, and so they carry on the Trade to their very great Profit and Advantage.

I need not add, that by the same navigation they receive all their heavy goods, as well such as are Imported at Hull, as such as come from London, and such as other counties supply, as butter, cheese, lead, iron, salt; all sorts of grocery, as sugars, tobacco fruit, speice, hops & c. oyl, wine, brandy, spirits and every sort of heavy of bulky goods.

The town of Leeds is very large, and, as above, there are abundance of wealthy merchants in it. Here are two churches, and two large meeting-houses of Dissenters, and six or seven chapels of ease, besides dissenters chapels, in the adjacent, depending villages; so that Leeds may not be much inferior to Hallifax in Numbers of people are thronged together in all the villages about these Towns, and how busy they all are, being fully employed in this great manufacture.

*c.***1730**

The *Leeds Intelligencer,* the major regional newspaper, was established by Griffith Wright in July 1754. He was probably the author of this poem, which was collected around 1839-50 from a manuscript in the possession of John Bishcoff. It gives a unique account of the everyday life of the local handloom weavers.

Griffith Wright — Matters of interest to the town of Leeds.
A Poem descriptive of the manners of the Clothiers.
Seated some hundred yards from Leeds
Crowded with those monstrous breeds,
Twining my bobin wheel among
The merry Clothiers' greasy throng
With wooden platter, bowl and ladle
All seated round a scowered table,
Hard oaten cakes, some two or three,
In peices fly, with fist and knee,
Tho' hard it in an instant doth
Eat like soft manchet (?) in the broth (?)
Ere Tom or Jack have supped their mess,
With quick large strides comes 'prentice Bess,
Who, on earthen dish, with leg of mutton,
As good as knife was ever put in —
Each cuts a lunch, none care to inch it —
'First come — first serv'd' — they never flinch it!
Nor use they many words at meat,
But cram like Capons, while they eat!
All rise well pleased with their cheer,
Then march to the spicket-Pot for beer.
When quench'd their thirst, they quickly go,
And thro' the web the shuttle throw.
Thus they keep time with hand and feet,
From five at morn till eight at *neet!*
Then call'd down e'er the clock gives warning,
Of (?) Broth is on the fire a-warming

Their wooden clogs like horses sound,
Beset the savoury wash-tub round.
Their (?) washing well ith' savoury tub,
It scowers well upon my word
Then *wrinceing* them in dish of water,
They comb their hair, and tie their garter,
And dried 'em on a tooel clean,
To supper then they all come in.
Master & Dame too being there,
Among the rest to take their share,
And while they're all at supper set,
Bess, a pan of water get,
And set in on the fire to heat,
To wash all clean, and keep all sweet.
Quoth Maister — 'Lads, work hard, I pray,
"Cloth mun be peark'd next market day,
"And Tom mun go to-morn to t'spinners,
"And will mun seek about for t'swingers;
"And Jack, tomorn, by time be rising,
"And go to th'sizing-house for sizing,
"And get your web, in warping, done
"That yet may get it into t'loom.
"Joe — go give my horse some corn
"For I design for t'wolds tomorn;
"So mind and clean my boots and shoon,
"For I'll be up it' morn right *soon!*
"Mary — there's wool — take' thee and dye it,
"It's that "at ligs i'th' cloated (?) sheet!"
Mistress: "So thou's setting me my wark,
"I think I'd more need mend they sack —
"Prithee, who mun sit at bobbin-wheel,
"And ne'er a cake at top o' the 'creel!
"And me to bake, and swing, and bend
"And milk, and bairns to school to send,
"And dumplins for the lads to make,
"And yeast to seek, and 'syk as that!"
"And washing up, morn, noon and neet,
"And bowls to scald, and milk to fleet,
"And bairns to fetch again at neet!"
Master: "When thou begins thou's never done!
"Bessy and thee mun get up soon,
"And stir about, and get all done —
"For all things mun aside be laid
"When we want help about our trade"
Wife: "Whey Bairn — we'll see what we can do
"but we hav' both to wesh and brew,
"And shall want Malt, Hops, Soap and Blue
"And thou'll be most a week away
"And I's hev'll t'wark folk to pay"
Master: "Let paying for their wark alone
"I'll pay'em all when I come home
"Keep t'lads at wark, and tak 'this purse,
"And set down what thou dost disburse,
"That we may not run hand ov'r head, —
"Bess says, we want some corn for bread,
"What fetch down t' meal that is i'th' ark,
"And let's get done before it's dark."
Bairnes in bed, and supper done,
And Bessy wash'd up dish and spoon,
Quoth Dame, 'come let us to Joe's,
"To talk, and hear how matters goes".
Dame and Maister out being gone,
Comes Will and Jack, and Joe & Tom,
Our neighbour Joey's lad and lass
In mirth an hour or so to pass.
All sitting round a good coal fire,
More free from care than Knight or Squire.

The 'bacco-box is then pull'd out,
For *chew,* and pipe to hand about.
Some fill their pipe, and some their lip
And all begin to take and *spit!*
Quoth Tom — "Lads, while ye all do quaff,
I'll tell yet what'll make 'ye laugh!
"To our house cam' one Sammy Shorty,
"To borrow our Maister's eight and forty!"
"We were throng teeming cloth at tenters,
"Maister were squeezing out swine-muck,
"Which was the cause of Sam's ill luck,
"For, standing close to t'maister's shoulder,
"Setting his foot upon a boulder,
"Pressing on't with all his might,
"Which caus'd the stone to take its flight,
"Leaving poor Sam, who straight did fall
"Into the tub of muck and all!
"Sammy aloud for help did call —
"Just in the nick of time came Hall,
"With a bag of *Saunders* on his back,
"Hearing the groan poor Sam did mack,
"Down bag of Saunders he did lie
"Upon a swinging truss hard by;
"The *hartshorn,* which from that did rise,
"Directly flew into his eyes,
"Which caused great pain, spite of resistance,
"Tho' both hands fly to their assistance.
"At length Sam from the tub did rush,
"And ran again' the swinging truss,
"Which made the poor man's head turn round
"And threw him flat upon the ground,
The truss'd Saunders following after —
"They all set up a roar of laughter!
"The bag burst open with the fall,
"And this upon poor Sam, did, all
"From head to foot him so be-spread,
"Quite changed his mucky hue to red —
"But he, by help of all, did rise,
"And fall to scrubbing of his eyes:
"Being almost spent with pain and toil,
"He staggering fell against the *coil.*
"Which showering down, like hail so thick
"Had not our Maister Hall been quick,
"He sure enough had there been slain —
"Howe'er they rais'd him sound again,
"And all way homeward as he went,
"He carried the savoury wash-tub scent, —
"Not only some thought him, but every
"Harry Groom, of *Stoles* in Livery,
"Being cover'd all with red and black,
"And the eight-and-forty on his back.
"Some that saw him, even Tom the Drovier,
"Swore that "Black Harry" was turned Clothier!" —
Thus they do themselves well please
With telling such like tales as these!
Or passing of a merry joke —
Till ten gives warning by the clock
And Bess set mending up her smock
Then up they start — to bed they run,
Maister and Dame home being come;
They sleep secure until the horn
Calls'em to work betimes i'th' morn;
Ere clock strikes eight they're called to breakfast,
And bowls to milk are brought in great haste —
Good Water — Pudding as heart could wish,
With spoons stuck round an earthen dish —
Maister gives orders to all in full,

Sets out to t'wolds, to buy his wool.
And while the good man is away,
The neighbour — wives all set a day
To meet, and drink a dish of tea!
With Dame, while she is left a widow,
As neighbours should — without being bid, you know.
"We ne'er stand knocking — Mistress, how do ye?
"Thank you and you — I am glad to see ye!
"Pray walk in, put off your things —
"Bess, get aforehand with the bobbins —
"Pray ye, walk into the other room,
"What stand ye for? come, set ye doon!
When they have sat and chat a while,
The kettle is brought in to boil,
The Tea-Table in order spread,
Rolls buttered, cold, and some toasted!
"Bohea or Green — mixed or clear?
"Which you please — do pray draw near!
So we will leave them at their ease,
And to discourse in what they please —
For to conclude I think it best,
And let my *Muse return to rest.*

From a MS in the possession of John Bischoff, Esq., Leeds.

*c.***1733**

Thomas Gent (1692-1778) of York was a prolific printer, writer, 'artist', and writer of doggerel. Restless in youth, argumentative in his middle years, and pathetic in the poverty of old age, his energy and enthusiasm for local history were beyond doubt. In numerous forays from his adopted city, he recorded massive amounts of information regarding Yorkshire's antiquities.
Gent, T. *A Journey into Some Parts of Yorkshire* (York 1733) p.34.

The Town of *Leeds* is really so beautiful, that, if ever I have an Opportunity, and can procure proper Materials, I shall set forth other Matters concerning it . . .How beautiful it is made by the River *Are,* the Bridge, the Schools, Market-Cross, the Guild-Hall adorn'd with a beautiful Effigy of Queen ANNE, with several other buildings both antient and modern: What fine Markets there are on Tuesdays and Saturdays for all the necessary Provisions to support Life, which begin at the sounding of a Bell, after so vast a Sale of their Cloth is over, that it would amaze any Person, to perceive how silently and calmly some Thousands of Pounds are laid out in that useful Commodity; how well the Poeple are govern'd, by the Prudence of its most worthy Magistrates; the latter made happy by the dutiful Obedience of the former: What a pious and learned Clergy, ever have done, and continue to adorn by their lives and Doctrines the decent churches that are contain'd therein. From all these Considerations, it may well be pronounc'd, To be a happy, pleasant and wealthy town, in every Respect most deservedly worthy of Celebration.

1743-54

George Bickham (1684-1758) of London was the author and engraver of many works on penmanship. Between 1743 and 1754 he and his son George jnr and John Bickham published *The British Monarchy,* a lavish combination of atlas, fine penmanship, and artistic illustration.
Bickham, G. *The British Monarchy* (1743) p.147:

This delightful woodcut from Thomas Gent's History of Ripon *shows Leeds from the south, its major features being the towers of St John's Church, Holy Trinity, and the parish church. On the extreme left, the manor house still stands within its moated enclosure on the site now occupied by The Scarborough public house in Bishopgate Street.*

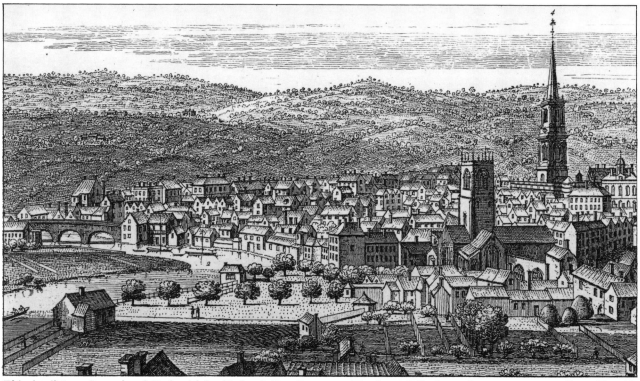

This detail from Samuel and Nathaniel Buck's South East Prospect of Leeds *of 1745 shows the town from Cavalier Hill, with Leeds Bridge to the left, and the parish church and holy Trinity towards the right. Note the orchards on Kirk Ing, between the parish church and the river and the haystacks and tenter-frames in the foreground.*

About Leeds was the first seat of the Cloathing Trade in England, and this Town is still remarkable for its Cloth-market, held every Tuesday and Saturday morning at Six a clock in summer, and Seven in Winter. Tho' vast Sums are here dealt for, ye Whole is always over in about an hour.

of the known World. There is besides the Market for mixt Cloth already mention'd, a handsome well built Hall for the White Cloth; under which are very convenient cells, where the Clothiers may deposit the cloth remaining unsold from one market day to another . . .

1745

Samuel Buck (1696-1779) first toured Britain as the topographical artist of the antiquary John Warburton (1661/2-1759), coming to Leeds and visiting Ralph Thoresby on 16 October 1719; the following description comes from the text accompanying the prospect of Leeds published by Samuel and his brother Nathaniel in 1745.
Buck, S. & N. *The South-East Prospect of Leeds* (1745).

. . .The market is allow'd to be the largest in England for Broad Cloths, which are exported from hence to Germany, Italy, Spain, Portugal, and even to the most remote places

1750

Richard Pococke (1704-1765) was a great traveller, touring France, Italy, Germany, Egypt, Palestine, Cyprus and Greece, as well as England, Scotland and Ireland. These observations of Leeds were made during his English tours of 1750-1752.
Pococke, Dr Richard 'Journey into England from Dublin by way of the Isle of Man, 1750' *Camden Society N.S* XLII (1888) pp.52-4.

I went six computed miles to Leeds, which is finely situated on the river Aire. A town of great trade in every branch of the woollen trade, but principally in clothes of the price of 2s 6d to 7s a yard. The market every Thursday and Saturday in summer at 6, in winter at 7 in the morning. On one side of the street, where four rows of forms are placed and extending about 200 yards in length, on which they have their cloth, and great sums are contracted for in one hour with very few words, the buyer asking the price, then bidding in answer, and the other then sets his price, and the buyer if he likes it, order it to be sent to such a place. A bell rings before the market begins, and to put an end to it, and this is a curiosity many people go to see. They have also a very fine market for all sorts of provisions, and especially the shambles are well-provided. I went to see three churches in the town. St John's was built by Mr John Harrison, alderman, whose picture is in the church. He built likewise a charity school, a free school, and a hospital for 40 people and died in 1651.

The new church is an handsome Dorick building with a spire. In St Peter's is buryed Thoresby the antiquarian, who writ the Autiquities of Leeds and died in 1729; but I found no account of the Savile family here as some books mention. I suppose by mistake. The coal pits come close to their houses; and there is a large fire engine for raising the water. This advantage and the great command they have of water is of great service to their manufactory . . .they have in this country from Skipton and on to the south-east a sort of causeway made of hewn free stone, about 18 inches broad and a yard long, which are laid across the ways so the road is but three feet wide and not very secure for horses not used to it, tho' nor apt to slip by reason of the soreness of the stone. On these they rise when the roads are bad, as they are in most parts after rain.

I visited Mr Wilson, the antiquarian, and went to visit another curious person, Dr Hilver, a physician, who was out of town. I went two miles above Leeds to Kirkstall Abbey, commonly called Cristall, founded in 1147 by Henry Lacy, Baron of Pontefract, for monks of the Cistertian Order, and dedicated to the Virgin Mary . . .

1755

In the mid eighteenth century, the streets of Leeds were becoming dangerous at night, when the darkness provided cover for robberies, burglaries, and other 'outrages and disorders'. To improve this situation, the following Act was obtained, by which a group of commissioners were enabled to raise local rates to provide street lighting.

An Act
For Enlightening the Streets and Lanes, and Regulating the Pavements in the Town of Leeds, in the County of York
(1755)

WHEREAS, the Town of Leeds, in the County of York, is a Place of great trade and large extent, consisting of many Streets, narrow lanes and alleys, inhabited by great numbers of Tradesmen, Manufacturers, Artificers, and others, who in the prosecution and carrying on their respective Trades and Manufacturers, are obliged to pass and repass through the same, as well in the night as in the day-time; And whereas several Burglaries, Robberies, and other Outrages and Discorders have lately been committed, and many more attempted within the said Town, and the Streets, Lanes, Alleys, and Passages thereof, and the enlightening the said Streets and Lanes, and regulating the Pavements thereof, would be of great advantage, and tend not only to the security and preservation of the Person and Properties of the Inhabitants of the said Town, but to the benefit and convenience of strangers and persons, resorting to the several markets kept within the said Town, and to others whose affairs may oblige them to pass and repass through the same, and also to prevent the many mischiefs which might happen as well from Fires, as Burglaries, Robberies and other Outrages and Disorders; Wherefore, for attaining, effecting, and carrying into execution the good ends and purposes aforementioned, May it please your Majesty that it may be enacted; and be it enacted by the King's most excellent Majesty, by and with the advice and consent of the Lords Spiritual and Temporal, and Commons in this present Parliament assembled, and by the authority of the same, that it shall and may be lawful to and for such of the inhabitants of the said Town of Leeds, as are by this Act charged and made charge-able, with and towards the Rates and Assessments hereby appointed to be raised and levied for the purpose of this act, to assemble and meet on the Twenty-fourth Day of June, One Thousand Seven Hundred and Fifty-five, between the Hours of ten of the clock in the morning and Two in the Afternoon, and on the first Wednesday in June, between the said Hours in every ensuing year, in the vestry of St Peter's church, commonly called the Old Church, in Leeds, aforesaid, and the said Inhabitants so assembled at their first Meeting shall then and there, and they are hereby required to nominate Fourteen of the principal inhabitants of the town of Leeds within the Bars, to be joined with the Mayor, Recorder, and Justices of the Peace, of the Borough and Town of Leeds aforesaid, for the time being, and who, together with the said Fourteen Persons so to be nominated, are hereby appointed Commissioners for putting this Act in Execution: and in case of the death or removal of any of the said Inhabitants so nominated, chosen or appointed, or their refusing to Act; it shall and may be lawful to and for the Inhabitants so qualified as aforesaid, to meet at the said Vestry Two Days Notice being always given for such Meetings, in the Church of St Peter's aforesaid, on the next preceding Sunday immediately after divine service, and then and there to nominate, elect, and appoint, other fit Persons Inhabiting within the Bars of the said town, to supply the place of such Persons as shall die, remove, or refuse to Act, to be joined with the Commissioners constituted and appointed to put this act in Execution; and such Person or Persons as shall from time to time be so elected and appointed, shall from thence-forth have the same power and authority to Act in all things relating to the matters herein contained, as if he or they had been expressly named in and appointed by this Act . . .

1756

Horace Walpole, (1717-1797) fourth Earl of Orford, was a author, wit, letter writer, collector and leader of the eighteenth century romantic taste for English 'Gothick'. He was one of the first of the fashionable visitors who came to Leeds to see the impressive ruins of Kirkstall Abbey.
Walpole, H. *Horace Walpole's correspondence.* vol.35 (Oxford University Press, 1973). *Letter to Richard Bentley from Wentworth Castle, August 1756.*

We crossed a Gothic bridge of eight arches at Ferrybridge, where there is a pretty view, and went to a large old house of Lord Huntingdon's at Ledstone, which has nothing remarkable but a lofty terrace, a whole-length portrait of his grandfather in tapestry, and the having belonged to the great Lord Stafford. We saw that monument of part of poor Sir John Bland's extravagance, his house and garden, which he left orders to make without once looking at either plan.

The house is a bastard Gothic, but of not near the extent I had heard. We lay at Leeds, a dingy large town; and through very bad black roads, for the whole country is a colliery, or a quarry, we went to Kirkstall Abbey, where are vast Saxon ruins, in a most picturesque situation , on the banks of a river that falls in a cascade among rich meadows, hills and woods: it belongs to Lord Cardigan: his father pulled down a large house here, lest it should interfere with the family seat, Deane.

1757

John Dyer (1900-1758) first studied art, but, following his return from Italy in the 1830s, he gave up painting, entered the church, and spent much of his time in writing and building. The following is a very brief extract from *The Fleece*, a poem which describes in considerable detail the process of manufacturing and marketting woollen cloth.
Dyer, J. 'The Fleece' (1757) in Johnson, S *Works of the English Poets* (1779) p.92.

Ruddy roofs, and chimney-tops appears,
Of busy Leeds, up-wafting to the clouds
The incease of thanksgiving: all is joy;
And trade an bufiness guide the living scene,
Roll the full cars, adown the winding Aire
Load the flow-sailing barges, pile the pack
On the long tinkling train of slow-pac'd steeds . . .

The creaking wain brings copious store of corn;
The grazier's sleeky kine obstruct the roads:
The neat-dress'd housewives, for the festal board
Crown'd with full baskets, in the field-way paths
Come tripping on; the echoing hills repear
The stoke of ax and hammer; scaffolds rise,
And growing edifices; heaps of stone,
Beneath and chissel, beauteous shapes assume
Of Frize and column. Some, with even line,
New streets are marking in the neighbouring fields,
And sacred domes of worship. Industry,
Which dignifies the artist, lifts and swaine,
And the straw cottage to a palace turns,

1760

'Tim Bobbin' was the pen-name of John Collier (1708-1768) of Lancashire, best known for his Lancashire dialect writings, and his robust paintings of everyday life in his native county. He spent most of his life as a master at Milnrow school, near Rochdale, but perhaps got his first-hand knowledge of Leeds merchants while serving as book-keeper for a cloth-manufacturer at Kebroyd in 1751. Fishwick, H. (ed) *The works of John Collier (Tim Bobbin)* (Rochdale 1894) p.237.

11 January 1760.

Leeds is a cunning but wealthy, thriving farmer. Its merchants hunt worldly wealth, as eager as dogs pursue the hare; they have, in general, the pride and haughtiness of *Spanish* dons, mixed with the meanness of *Dutch* spirits; the strong desire they have of yellow dirt (gold), transforms them into galley-slaves, and their servants are doubly so; the first being fastened with golden, but the latter with iron chains.

1767

The Revd. Joseph Ismay (1708-1778) was vicar of Mirfield from 1740 up to the time of his death. In this description of a visit to 'Mr B.T.' (the Rev Benjamin Tidswell of Chapel Allerton), he meets 'Mr R.' (the clothier John Rogerson), who provided detailed information on the building and trade of the Coloured Cloth Hall. Ismay, Revd. J. 'A Journal in May, 1767' *Thoresby Scoiety XXXVII* (Leeds 1945), pp.335-9.

May 12. We set out from Mirfield about seven o'clock in ye morning, went thro' Birstall, and arrived at Leeds about ten; I alighted at the George in Briggate, where I met the Rev.Mr B.T. We drank a Glass or two of white Wine and Bitters and then with our Friend Mr R. took a view of ye Market House for coloured cloth, which is a spacious, grand Building, and perhaps the largest Cloth Hall in Europe. It cost £5,248 and measures in length 160 yards. It contains 199 Windows, 4 yards high, and 5 feet wide. There are five long apartments, viz. King's Street 66 yards long — Queen's Street — Change Alley — Mary's Lane and Cheapside. This House was built in such a position as entirely prevents the rays of ye sun or a blaze of Light entering ye Apartments, either in ye Winter or Summer Season till after ye Time appointed for ye cloth's being exposed to sale. They could not shew the Cloth in a true Light if the sun was suffored to shine upon it.
  The Market was over when we entered this magnificent Hall, and all ye Apartments were visited by ye solar Rays. The echo repeated the sound ten Times, and our friend R. who was the chief Director and Manager in erecting this

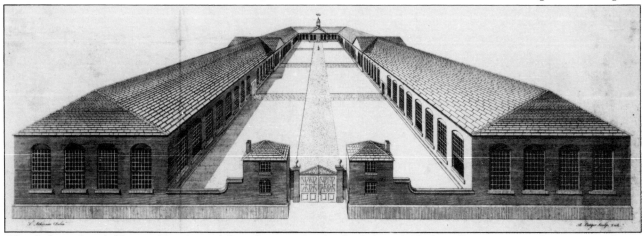

The cloth markets held every Tuesday and Saturday morning in the Coloured Cloth Hall were one of the greatest sights of late eighteenth-century Leeds, virtually every traveller commenting on their size and efficiency. This engraving shows the hall as it was built in 1758, when it occupied the area of the present City Square, General Post Office and Cloth Hall Court.

celebrated Building, told us that there were no less than 9,040 Pieces in ye Hall at that Juncture, besides what had been sold in ye morning.

We viewed ye House, Gardens and Canal of R.Wilson Esqr. Recorded of this town, and then returned to the Inn.

Leeds is a large, wealthy and populous Town, standing on ye North side of the River Aire with great suburbs on the south side, and both joined by a very large strong stone Bridge. Here are three churches, several meeting Houses, and two Cloth Halls, and several neat and superb Buildings for ye Merchants. There are about 5,000 Families in ye Township, as appears by a late survey, made at ye Expense of ye present Vicar Dr Kirkshaw.

From Leeds we proceeded to Chapel-Allerton, where I intended to spend a few Days with my Friend Mr T. who is Minister at that place. We dined about one, smoaked a Pipe, drank Tea, and then walked to the Bowling Green, where we passed two or three hours with some military Gentlemen from Leeds in a very pleasant, agreeable manner. A Gentleman and his Lady supped and spent the Evening with us at my Friend's House.

Wed. May 13 My Friend's House is pleasantly situated upon an eminence by ye Turnpike road and commands a very extensive Prospect. I could see from my Chamber Window five Churches, viz 3 at Leeds, Whitchurch and Pontefract. We drank Coffee in the morning, and then went to view my Friend's Chapel, which is a neat Building, and well seated. It is worth 93£ per annum. The Pew Rents amount to 30£ annually, Surplice Dues, and some considerable Augmentations made to it by obtaining Queen Anne's Bounty make up the Stipend or Salary independent of ye People.

Chapel-Allerton is two miles north of Leeds and pleasantly situate on ye skirts of a fine green Waste or Moor. There are a long Range of good neat Buildings on each side of the Common with a spacious Plain carpet Ground between each row of Houses. The South side is called *Potter-Newton*, and the North *Chapel-Allerton*. The most noted Buildings are Lawyer Barker's good old Mansion, with a long Avenue of Trees planted on ye Waste, which forms a beautiful Lawn up to ye House. The new House of Jeremiah Dixon Esq on black Moor, Mr Oats's Houses, particularly that on ye North side, which is an elegant Box with neat Gardens and pleasant Walks enclosed with Palisadoes to a small Farm House, where ye Poultry, etc., are kept. We saw white turkeys at this place, which, it seems, are much in Fashion at present; but Fashions in England seldom last long. Both black and white turkeys, we are informed, are found in the Phillipine Islands, with red heads; and therefore in all probability when ye white Turkeys become common, they will be succeeded by ye black Breed.

The Gentlemen and Ladies from Leeds frequently make an Excursion, either on Horseback or in their Chaises, to Chapel Town, in order to enjoy fresh Air upon this moor in ye Mornings, that they may eat their Dinner with a keener appetite, and a better Relish at ye return.

This village may, I think, be called the Montpelier of Yorkshire. There is a very good Inn at ye Bowling Green, and excellent Accomodations Three Clubs are held at this place, viz one for bowling, another for cricket, and a third which is called Lascelles Club. The Woolen Manufacture seems to terminate about this Town. The sand used in this village is brought from black Moor, and is of a yellowish colour. Abotu ten o'clock we set out for Harwood, we passed Moor Town; Moor Grange, and rode over black Moor, pursuing ye Turnpike Road.

1768

Arthur Young (1741-1820), farmer and writer on agricultural improvements, made a tour of 21 northern and midland counties in 1768, noting the current state of agriculture, houses, gardens and other relevant objects of interest.
Young, A. *Six months Tour Through North of England* (1770) vol.I. p.136-8.

The country between Wakefield and Leeds continues very beautiful but the roads stony and very ill made. At this town, but more in the neighbourhood, is carried on a vast manufacturing trade: Leeds Cloth market is well known, and has often been described. They chiefly make broad cloths from 1s 8d. a yard to 12s. but mostly of 4s 6d and 5s. Good hands at this branch, would earn about 10s 6d a week the year round, if they were fully employed, but as it is, cannot make above 8s. The difference of 2s 6d is a melancholy consideration. A boy of 13 or 14 about 4s a week, some women earn as much by weaving as much as the men. The men, at what they call offal work, which is the inferior branches, such as picking, rinking & c are paid 1d an hour. Besides broad cloths, there are some shalloons and many stuffs made at Leeds, particularly Scotch camblets, grograms, turckies, some callimancoes and &c. The weavers earn from 5s to 12s a week; upon an average 7s. Boys of 13 or 14, 5s a week. But they are all thrown out in bad weather, men in general at an average the year round, about 6s 6d a week. They never want for work at weaving. Dressers earn from 1s to 3s a day but are much thrown out by want of work. The women by weaving shifts earn 3s 6d or 4s a week. Wool combers 6s to 12s a week. The spinning trade is constant, women earn about 2s 6d or 3s a week. Girls of 13 or 14 earn 1s 8d a week. A boy of 8 or 9 ditto 2½d a day; of 6 years old 1d a day. The business of this town flourished greatly during the war, but sunk much at peace and continued very languid till within these two years when it began to rise again.

1771

Tate Wilkinson (1739-1803) began his acting career at Covent Garden in 1757, but then moved to York in 1766, where he became a great actor-manager, mounting performances in York, Hull, Newcastle, Halifax, Doncaster, Beverley, Sheffield, Wakefield and Leeds.
Wilkinson, T. *The Wandering Patentee: or, a history of the Yorkshire theatres, from 1770 to the present time . . .(1795) The Theatre was in Hunslet Lane.*

I will now adjourn from the assizes at York, 1771, to the opening of Leeds Theatre, Wednesday July 24, of the same year. The play was "A word to the Wise" with Mr Murphy's farce of "What we must all come to". The Theatre was built very neat-aye, and very splendid, comparatively speaking to the very mean places, such as the barns, warehouses, and &c to which they had been accustomed. However, with the help of good scenery, wardrobe, and in truth, a very excellent company, with a various and strong catalogue of plays, the houses were well attended, and gave hopes that the seeds of promise were sown and would produce a plentiful harvest and a lasting produce. Four weeks only as manager was my first experiment. I was not aided then or since by much assistance as to personal connexions there, but am from long intercourse well known by everybody as to general acquaintance; and if I wanted credit in any tradesman's books, have not the least doubt but I might pay myself the compliment to declare, that not any shop would refuse, but be glad to the custom of Tate Wilkinson, manager of the

Leeds Theatre. But at that period it was not so; for the inhabitants not being accustomed to any players of tolerable credit, and the lower order having suffered greatly by the depredations of dishonesty, and perhaps real distress and penury in the extreme, made every one shy of giving credit or countenance; which was rather strange, considering the vicinity of the opulent town of Leeds to the city of York. As to patrons I had none, and was an entire stranger, except to Alderman Kenyon and his lady, who were at that time particularly kind, not only as to constant friendly invitations, but were also strenuous props to the Theatre at the necessary juncture, never failing in their due attendance for mine and the company's welfare.

Past kindnesses should never be forgot, as indeed at that time neither the wind, the rain, nor the weather ever kept Mr or Mrs Kenyon from the Theatre; and whenever I despaired of success, I well remember Mr Kenyon remarked and prophesied, that in time, with perseverance and tolerable attention to the entertainment of the public, the town of Leeds would be held more lucrative and respectable in the opinion of players than I then seemed to apprehend.

The generous and friendly Mr Barstow (then Town-Clerk of Leeds) of truly respectable memory, had a hand as open as day, as likewise Mrs Barstow, his first wife, who I can really aver was sincere and friendly to Mrs Wilkinson, me, and mine: Indeed Mr Barstow's house ever had the hinges ready to fly and open the friendly doors to let me in, even at any hour, and my hours (unless to a Londoner) were then as now, very strange; nad notwithstanding it is an evil habit, yet to me it is luxurious, even though assured without a lecturer, that the practice hurts my health, which is not as a lusty winter. My wine is often rebellious; by the bye the reader must understand I am not by any means a drunken man, but from accident (almost now and then unavoidable) I live more freely than my stomach and health would permit, were strict prudence the guide. Indeed I by no means dislike the chimney-corner of life, particularly where that corner affords me every necessary. There was a gentleman, *at that time*, whom I likewise esteemed as a great support to the Leeds theatre; I *now* return him thanks for his former kindness.

1777

Samuel Curwen (1715-1802) was a merchant at Salem, new Jersey, USA, who migrated to England to avoid harassment for his loyalist views. A contemporary writer described him as 'an excellent Antiquarian . . .a good Classical Latin Scholar, well read in History. had conversed much with men, was much of a gentleman . . .The English tye Wig, the long Scarlet Cloak, the heavy rings, and the golden headed cane . . .'.
Oliver, A. (ed.) *The Journal of Samuel Curwen Loyalist* (Harvard Univ.Press 1972) vol II p.359-60.

Saturday 31 (May 1777).

Having ordered a servant with Mr Russell's and Curwen's compliments to S.Elam we waited for breakfast; he soon came but declined to partake, having before taken his, but after conversation and an hearty welcome to this town we walk forth accepted his invitation to dinner passed the P.M. in his company, drank tea with him, and rambled about and a village called Armley to see a scribbling mill by which more wool is discharged at once than 10 hands can do; tis performed by an horse, its peculiar construction cant be described as it is not exposed to openview, it being a favour with a sight of it, too nice an inspection would have excited

suspicion we were to avoid. The manufacturers of every kind thro' England are not pleased to admit strangers to a sight of their machines, and the process of their business. From thence we returned back in company with Mr Elam who invited us to dine next day, at the side of the canal, which for the first time is to be opened with some ceremony next Wednesday. No part of it has hitherto been used. Passed the evenings at lodgings.
Monday June 2 1777.

This town is said to contain ten thousand people, many well-filled shops, and various trades; its principal business in narrow and coarse woollen cloths, consigned to foreign orders, but little to London or inland trade; many of its merchants are wealthy. It has a large cloth market made of brick of three ranges, each range having two walks, and the walks are called King-Street, Cheapside, Queen-street etc.

1779

James Boswell (1740-1795) is best known for his biography of Dr Samuel Johnson, but he also produced poems, political essays, travelogues and a number of articles in the *London Journal*. He visited Leeds in the company of Lt.Col.James Stuart in the early autumn of 1779. Regettably his journal has been lost, but at least we know his opinion of the Leeds Library.

London Magazine January 1782, p.268.

"In Leeds, where one would not expect it, there is a very good public library, where strangers are treated with great civility, of which I for one retain a grateful sense. I there found a manuscript containing the coats of arms and descents of the families of the West Riding of Yorkshire, upon which there is this inscription, which I copied as highly expressive of a true devotee to a Museum: "Every ingenious fragment is venerable to the Virtuoso, and always pleasant to a curious inquisitive mind. But a collector should have the industry of a Hercules; and the patience of a Socrates; an eye like Argus; and a purse like Cresus."

1788

Charles Dibdin (1745-1814) was a dramatist and songwriter, and a skilled singer and a performer on keyboard instruments. In 1787 he commenced a fourteen-month tour of various towns, promoting concerts at which he was the sole performer. This description was made during the course of this tour.
Dibdin, C. *The musical tour of Mr Dibdin (1788)*.

Leeds is a town of great trade; so much so, that a gentleman belonging to one of the banks assured me the whole returns of the place could not be less than from five to seven millions a year. This cannot be done but by men who have thrown *fortunes* into *trade*, who, as I have often experienced, have nothing of the littleness that springs in low minds from *turning the penny*. I desire also I may not be understood to say that there are not tradesmen who have heads and hearts that would do honour to the highest situations. *Kings* may do *little* actions, and *coblers* — *great* ones. I aim at nothing but to distinguish between meanness and generosity. Those who possess — and that largely — the latter quality, are now among Mr Warburton's friends; and I fancy any man, upon the same terms, will not feel uneasy at being — in the way he is *out of favour*. Such favour is as indifferent to him, as yours is material to.

Dear Sir,

Your obliged friend,

C.Dibdin

Sheffield, 4 March 1788.

1795

Dr John Aiken (1747-1822) was better known as a man of letters than as a physician. His elegant scholarship gave a natural polish to all he wrote, which included biographies, translations of classical authors, and topography, including the volume from which this extract is taken.

Aikin, J. *A Description of the Country from Thirty to Forty Miles Around Manchester* (London 1795) p.570-577.

Leeds

Though the woollen trade in Yorkshire has properly no one common centre, yet the town of Leeds has latterly been always reckoned, in opulence and population, the principal place of the West Riding; and it bears a high rank among our manufacturing towns.

Leeds is an ancient place, its name appearing in Doomsday book, under the reigns of Edward the Confessor and William the Conqueror. It had a strong castle, probably built by Ilbert de Lacy, which was besieged by King Stephen in 1139; and here the unfortuante Richard II was confirmed about the year 1399. No vestiges of this fortress remain; but its site is said to have been on a place now called Mill-Hill.

Leeds has long been distinguished as one of the cloathing towns of Yorkshire, though its pre-eminence does not seem to have been of very old date. Leland says it is "a pretty market town, subsisted chiefly "by cloathing, reasonably well builded, and as large as Bradford, "but not so quick as it".

Its growth, however, probably soon came to be considerable, as it was incorporated by Charles I. At the commencement of the troubles of that reign it was held for the king by Sir William Saville; but after a sharp action, its works were stormed by a force which marched out of Bradford under Sir Thomas Fairfax. A second charter was given to it in the 13th of Charles II, under which it is now governed. it is not a parliamentary borough.

The parish of Leeds is situated on the river Aire, which runs nearly through the middle of it in a direction from west to east. It extends, according to Tuke's survey, seven miles three furlongs from north to south, and seven miles two and half furlongs from east to west, and is thirty miles one furlong in circumference. It is divided into ten townships, exclusive of the township of Leeds, which includes the town properly so called, and a considerable cillage at a mile's distance. An actual enumeration of the inhabitants of the township was taken in 1775, of which the following is the result: families 4099; husbands, 3121; wives 3193; widowers, 347; widows 793; females ditto, 3760; spinsters 1330; males under twenty-one 3712; females ditto, 3760; total, 17,117; number of each family, $4^1/_5$. It is to be observed, that in the lowest rank of people there is often more than one family to a house. In that year there was 1140 baptisms, and 781 burials.

The living is a vicarage in the gift of twenty-seven trustees, who previous to a presentation, are required to complete their number by the votes of a majority of the survivors. The profits of the living arise entirely from small tithes and Easter dues, and are said to be short of £.400 per annum, though they would certainly be much more if the dues were rigorously exacted. Besides the parish church, there are in the town three other churches: two of these are supported by handsome endowments of land, and are in the gift of trustees; the other, lately erected, by the sale and rent of pews,

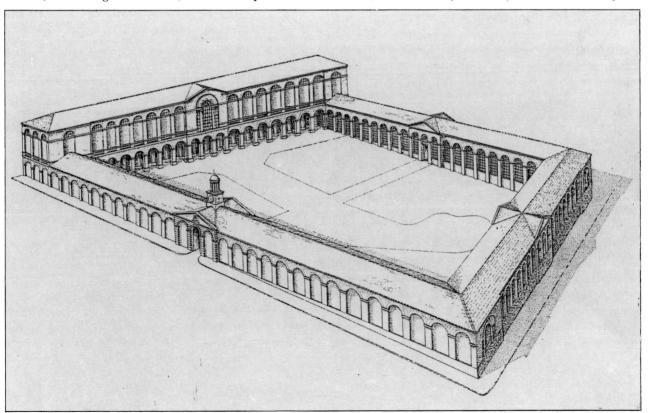

The third White Cloth Hall of 1775 was built in the form of a large rectangle on a former tenter field extending from the Calls almost as far as Kirkgate. In 1776-7 the northern wing was extended in width and height in order to create one of the most elegant assembly rooms in England. Here the local merchants and gentry met for the balls, concerts and card games which played such an important part in their social life.

and after two presentations is to be in the gift of the vicar. Eight of the ten townships have an episcopal endowed chapel of ease, in the gift of the vicar, and are upon an average worth about £.100 per annum each. These are also in the town seven dissenting-meeting houses, viz two Presbyterian, two Independant, two Baptist, and one Quaker's exclusive of a large chapel belonging to the Westley methodists, and of another where the service of the church of England is read by two unordained preachers, educated at the expence of the late countess of Huntingdon.

The parish is governed by a corporation, consisting of a mayor, twelve aldermen, and twenty-four common council, who fill up the vacancies in their body, and annually elect the mayor from the aldermen by a majority of votes. As there are no freemen, every inhabitant is eligible to serve in the corporation, and in return is not liable to be summoned to serve upon any jury out of the parish.

The market days are Tuesday and Saturday for mixed cloths, that is, cloths made of dyed wool; and Tuesday only, for white cloths. The mixed cloths in the last century were exposed for sale on the battlements of the bridge over the Aire, and as the manufactory increased, were removed to the large street called Briggate, subject to the inconvenience of bad weather, and of being stored in adjoining cellars from one market day to another. The white cloths were sold in a room. Each of them is now deposited in a separate covered hall, erected for the purpose, where they remain without disturbance till sold.

The mixed cloth hall was erected at the expense of the manufacturers in 1758. It is a quadrangular building, enclosing an open area. The building is 127½ yards in length, and sixty-six in breadth, and is divided into six covred streets, each of which contains two rows of stands, the freehold property of separate manufacturers. Each stand is twenty-two inches in front, and the whole number is 1770; but as about twenty individuals are in possession of two stands each, the number of master manufacturers of mixed cloth, proprietors of the hall, must not be estimated at more than 1750. These have all served a regular apprenticeship to the making of coloured cloth, which is an indispensable condition of their admission into the hall. Another small hall has lately been erected for the accommodation of irregulars, and near 100 stands are already let. Each stand originally cost the proprietor £1.5s 6d., but they are now worth 51.10s.

The present white cloth hall was built in 1775. It is a quadrangle like the other, ninety-nine yards in length, and seventy in breadth, and is divided into five streets, each with a double row of stands, the number of which is 1210; but there are generally about forty persons who have two stands each. There are supposed to be about 200 mixed, and more than 100 white cloth manufacturers, of an inferior description, who have served a regular apprenticeship, but having no property in the halls, pay a fixed fee for every piece of cloth they expose to sale.

The whole number of master broad-cloth manufacturers, in the west-riding of Yorkshire is about 3240. The mixed cloth manufacturers reside partly in the villages belonging to the parish of Leeds; but chiefly at Morley, Guildersome, Adwalton, Dringlington, Pudsey, Farsley, Calverley, Eccleshal, Idle, Baildon, Yeadon, Guiseley, Rawdon and Horsforth, in or bordering upon the vale of Aire, chiefly west of Leeds; and at Batley, Dewsbury, Osset, Horbury and Kirkburton, west of Wakefield, in or near the vale of Calder. Not a single manufacturer is to be found more than one mile east, or two north, of Leeds; nor are there many in the town of Leeds, and those only in the outskirts.

The white cloth is manufactured chiefly at Alverthorpe, Osset, Kirkheaton, Dewsbury, Batley, Birstal, Hopton, Mirfield, Archet, Clackheaton, Littletown, Bowling and Shipley; a tract of country forming an oblique belt across the hills that separate the vale of Calder from the vale of Aire, beginning about a mile west of Wakefield, leaving Huddersfield and Bradford a little to the left, terminating at Shipley on the Aire, and not coming within less than about six miles of Leeds on the right. The districts of the white and coloured cloth manufactory are generally distinct, but are a little intermixed at the south-east and north-west extremities.

The cloths are sold in their respective halls rought as they come from the fulling mills. They are finished by the merchants, who employ dressers, dyers and c. for that purpose; these, with drysalters, shop-keepers, and the different kind of handicraftmen common to every town, compose the bulk of the inhabitants of Leeds. The dispersed state of the manufacturers in villages and single houses over the whole face of the country, is highly-favourable to their morals and happiness. They are generally men of small capitals, and often annex a small farm to their other business; great numbers of the rest have a field or two to support a horse and a cow, and are for the most part blessed with the comforts, without the superfluities, of life.

The markets of Leeds are well supplied with all kinds of provision, partly from the neighbouring agricultural district to the east, and partly from a distance up the Aire. The whole country from Leeds westward into Lancashire, does not produce grain or feed cattle sufficient to supply one-fifth of the inhabitants.

The medium price of the best beef is from fivepence to sixpence per pound; mutton and veal fourpence halfpenny; pork, sixpence; upon an average, about a halfpenny a pound dearer than York, and as much cheaper than Manchester.

Leeds has a general infirmary, built by subscription in 1768, and well attended and supported. Also an excellent workhouse, an hospital, alms-houses, charity schools, and other institutions belonging to a great town. It is built of brick, and contains many large and handsome modern houses. From the beginning of the century Leeds has enjoyed the benefit of water-carriage by means of the river Aire, which has been improved by successive acts, the last of which, authorizing a canal from the lower part of the Aire to the Ouse at Selby, passed in 1774.

Its population has kept pace with the general increase of the cloathing trade, as will appear from the following extract from the bills of mortality:

An account of the births and burials in the township of Leeds from 1763 to 1794, including protestant dissenters of all denominations:

Year	Births	Bur	Year	Births	Bur
1764	553	445	1773	699	660
1765	576	459	1774	630	478
1766	584	533	1775	705	574
1767	557	639	1776	712	475
1768	552	560	1777	710	634
1769	637	478	1778	781	656
1770	621	587	1779	709	686
1771	689	533	1780	742	591
1772	650	544	1781	738	573
1782	741	600	1788	933	784
1783	725	682	1789	993	671
1784	830	608	1790	1139	969
1785	860	727	1791	1142	688
1786	940	674	1792	1171	929
1787	895	712	1793	1190	1129

Number of houses in the year 1793, counted from the workhouse book, where all that are inhabited are inserted, 6,691.

The soil of the parish of Leeds is a coarse, strong clay, sometimes covering a finer stratum, which is made into pipes, and an inferior kind of pottery, in the neighbourhood. Its northern border is sandy, extending nearly to the ridge which separates Airedale from Wharfdale, and is a process from the great line of hills that form a back bone of the north of England. The higher part of it is incapable of cultivation. That part of the parish which lies south of the Aire abounds in coal; and to the cheapness of this indispensable mineral, the flourishing state of the manufactory is to be attributed. It is delivered at the coal staith in the town, at 13s per waggon load. The waggon is supposed to contain twenty-four corves, and the weight of a corve is near two hundred weight and a half.

There are in the parish several quarries of an argillaceous schift, which supply the neighbourhood and the country down the river with slates and flag-stones for paving. On the north-east border begins a bed of imperfect granite, or moor-stone, of the same kind as that on the east moor in Derbyshire, which runs to the Chevin near Otley, and forms the whole ridge of Romald's-moor as far as Skipton, where the line-stone commences. On each side, as you approach the level of the rivers Aire and Wharfe, the argillaceous schift occurs, which is evidently a stratum incumbent on the granite. The stone on the south of the Aire is entirely argillaceous schift, as probably is generally the case where coal is found. The land in the greater part of the parish is extremely rich, and on account of the plenty of manure and the populousness of the country, is of course in a high state of cultivation.

Besides the smaller potteries which work up the low stratum of clay, there is a very considerable one for pottery of a finer kind, the proprietors of which, on account of the cheapness of coal, find it worth their while to bring pot clay and flints from the west and south of England, and export large quantities of goods to Holland, Germany, Russia, &c.

There are also in the town two carpet manufactories; and a large work has lately been erected for spinning flax by machinery.

On the river Aire and the streams that fall into it, there are numberous mills for grinding corn, dyer's-wood, rape feed, &c. and also for fulling cloth, and turning machinery to spin and card wool. Several cotton mills have been lately erected, but these are worked chiefly by the means of steam engines.

1795

Henry Skrine (1755-1803) spent most of his time travelling throughout Great Britain, his observations being published in three major books issued in 1795, 1798 and 1801.
Skrine, H. *Three Successive Tours in the North of England* (1795) IX.

Leeds . . .seems to want the neatness and regularity which prevail at Wakefield. We had an opportunity of visiting its cloth hall during the market, which fills three sides of a spacious quadrangle, forming two long galleries, which communicate in several places with each other, and join at the end so as to encompass the whole building. Here an innumerable quantity of cloths are ranged on each side, on a row of tables by which the manufacturers stand, with little rods or brushes in their hands, ready to deal with the chapmen, who are diligent in examining the goods, and

transact everything in a whisper. The novelty of the scene both surprised and interested us; and the size of the building, though much inferior to Halifax, which we afterwards visited, far exceeded our expectations.

1797

Sir Frederick Eden (1766-1809) was a pioneer in the field of social and economic investigations, his major achievement being a study of the labouring population of England in the 1790s, carried out both by personal visits, and by the evidence provided by a large number of correspondents.
Eden, Sir F. *The State of the Poor* (1797) p.358-9.

Leeds contains about 4,000 acres, of which 30 are waste, and about 31,500 inhabitants. In 1775 the population was 17,117. 1,836 houses pay tax, 4,866 are exempt. Rent of land is high, £2 to £5 an acre. Land in the skirts of the town frequently sells for £300 an acre, and some times for £1,000. Prices of provisions; Oatmeal, 2s 3d per stone of 14lbs; flour, 2s 3½d to 2s 5½d per stone; beef 3½d to 5½d per lb; mutton and veal, 4½d; port 4d; bacon 7d; milk 2d per quart; butter, 11d for 16oz; potatoes, 11d per peck, Winchester measure. Wheaten bread is generally used. Some is made partly of rye and a few persons use oatmeal. Animal food forms a considerable part of the diet of labouring people. Tea is now the ordinary breakfast, especially among women of every description, and the food of both men and women is more expensive than that consumed by persons in the same station of life in the more northern parts. Many persons complain that the introduction of machinery for spinning and carding wool not only deprive the industrious poor of employment, but are a great national disadvantage. But the high price of land and water, the many new streets in the town, and the manufactories and villas in the neighbourhood are a very convincing proof of the prosperity of Leeds.

1799

Robert Brown (1757-1831), a native of southern Scotland, was both editor of the Edinburgh *Farmer's magazine* and an extensive writer on agricultural science. This passage comes from his survey of the West Riding of Yorkshire carried out for the board of Agriculture.
Brown, R. *General View of the Agriculture of the West Riding of Yorkshire* (Edinburgh, 1799) Appendix 1, p.12-14.

Arrived at Leeds. Leeds is situated on the river Aire. It is a very ancient, and populous town, and was of considerable repute during the Saxon government. The woollen manufactory has flourished here for several ages, which has both enriched the inhabitants, and increased the value of the land in the neighbourhood.

The following is the most accurate accounts we could procure of the state of husbandry near Leeds.

The soil variable — a great part of it good, generally loam upon a clay bottom. Climate dry. Land possessed by small proprietors, and mostly occupied by manufacturers; a few of what are here called large farmers, having from 100 to 150 acres of land. Land employed partly in pasture, partly in meadow, and a proportion in tillage, but ought all to be in grass upon account of the great demand from Leeds for milk. Some clover and rye-grass sown. The stock kept upon the pastures are cows and horses belonging to manufacturers. Part of the land watered and turns out well. Grains cultivated are wheat, barley, oats and beans; also some rape, and turnips, which are generally sown broadcast. A few beans are drilled. Fallowing much practised. Large quantities of potatoes raised, and a great demand for them. Much time is used, and both grass, and fallow dunged. An excellent manure is got from the sizing boiler's waste which is the bones and remains of sheep's feet, cow's feet, and sloughs of horns. Horses only used, Seed time, and harvest early. Land mostly inclosed, and rents greatly increased thereby. Inclosures from 5 to 8 acres, and the smallest ones most valuable, being possessed by clothiers, who have no use for large ones. Inclosing in a manufacturing county must increase population . . .

Roads in general but tolerable, owing to their being let to undertakers, who neglect them. Houses for manufacturers well constructed: and a great many more wanted . . .

1799-1801

John Russell RA (1745-1806) painter to the King, the Prince of Wales, and the Duke of York, spent a considerable period in Leeds at the turn of the eighteenth century, where he made excellent pastel or

oil portraits of its leading citizens, including members of the Gott, Marshall, Sheepshanks, Lloyd and Cookson families.
Williamson, G.C. *John Russell R.A.* (1894) p.63-8.

Streets are named gates in this town, as Kirkgate, Briggate, etc: a bridge is called Brig. Briggate seems to be the principal street of trade with shops. The Town Hall and Market Cross are in it. On Market days in the shambles in this street, fruit, poultry etc. are exhibited in great abundance and it is arranged like Fleet Market, to which it bears a resemblance . . .November 8. The fair was held at Leeds this day, the shops were shut up, as it was for cattle. The whole of Briggate was filled, it was dangerous to pass, and droves passing other streets filled the whole town with bustle. November 9th was the Toy Fair. A few irregular stalls with cakes etc was all I saw, with clowns who I could not understand. Young women and men offering themselves for service stood about, to be hired for the year. This was a curiosity to me, but I saw not much to gratify expectation . . .To the common people here I seem as a barbarian, and they to me. Their speech I can't, without difficulty, understand. I asked a man in the street where a person lived and his answer was 'I cannot understand'. The young people look cheerful, the

The Moot Hall, or Town Hall, stood in the centre of Briggate, just above its junction with Kirkgate. Behind its elegant frontage, erected in 1710, the shambles, or butchers' shops, extended back to the pillared market cross, which can be seen in the distance in this view by Thomas Taylor. This whole block was swept away in 1825, in order to prevent further congestion in Briggate.

women rather pretty, with round faces, and of a good colour; but when I hear them speak, I feel surprised at the different selection and pronunciation of words. I do not hear the evil language in the streets of Leeds as in London. I have not heard an oath, nor have I been witness to an immoral action. This place is very remarkable in respect to religion, and what is more so, that amongst the rich and great a very considerable body are devout, approve and receive the gospel. The Methodist societies are very large and extend to all the villages and town adjacent. They do not seem to run into the American views so much in this town; are more useful and pious of consequence. Most of them attend the gospel preached here in the churches, having no meetings open in the time of service in the establishment. The Dissenters here seem of a much better spirit and on a better plan than in other places have seen. But there is a Socinian Meeting, where, in general, the members are like other Socinians, and what can say worse? For my part I hope to continue thankful for the Bible and the Church of England. The more I see of sects and parties the more I feel myself confirmed in the church . . .

The old and mother church, St Peter's, is a very large Gothic respectable structure with mixture of the heavy Saxon architecture. It stands in a large churchyard, filled with stones, evidencing the largeness of Leeds and its population. The church is not without external ornaments, but it has no claim to delicacy from its pinnacles, as they are but decently introduced. The stone is rough, and rather of a dark brown tint; but, however, the whole is very respectable, and from its vastness had an additional grandeur . . . St Peter's is a Vicarage, a large house is belonging to the Vicar in Kirkgate. Rev. Mr Atkinson is the lecturer . . .

I have, since I mentioned St Peter's Church, seen inside of it, which is spacious indeed, the chancel is impressively large. It receives over 100 communicants, in it there are pews for their accommodation, all the Ministers in the town help to administer on occasion. It is crowded with monuments and banners and escutcheons which do not incommode, as they lie upon the ground, or hang upon the walls and pillars . . .

St Peter's Square is large but not elegant, although the houses are new. St James's Church, not far from this square, is a new building, not so large as St Paul's but it is commodious and well fitted. The minister is the Rev. Mr King . . .

Park Place is a fine large row of elegant houses, new, extremely neat, large and well-built. The rooms inside are as elegant as on the outside, and by far the best part of Leeds, near the new church of St Paul's, which is a large and fine church. Rev. Watkins is the minister of it . . .

St John's Church is situated in the new street, Rev. Mr Sheepshanks the minister, a very considerable astronomical gentleman, with whom I spent an evening at Mr Hey's.

The Trinity Church is an elegant structure situated in Boar Lane.

The custom at the sacrament is peculiar perhaps to this place in the churches. The communicants keep their pews the whole time, and the ministers bring the elements round to each person. At funderals, they carry the coffin in) a solemn manner with towels underneath, passing from one to the opposite person, and not raised far from the ground . . .

I saw the Sunday Schools on the moor near Woodhouse, about 100 boys, in the other about as many girls; they seem well conducted, and are under the immediate inspection of Mr Sawyer, who took me to see them . . . the number of boys and girls thus restrained in Leeds amount to 2,000 and I understand, are carefully attended to by religious persons, consequently well conducted. The number of mills in Leeds

and vicinity surprised me, both of wind and water. They grind corn, oil, dyer's materials etc. The river is large, black, and nasty, which arises most probably from the dyes and filth from manufactories. (In the coloured cloth hall) as the dealers who come to purchase pass in the alleys between, they strike the cloth with the palms of their hands, each man to draw attention to his bale of goods. I was much struck with the sharp lookout they had for custom; the ardent look of the eye and the stroke upon their cloth was chiefly their means of asking in the Hall. (In the White Cloth Hall) the sellers of cloth lean over their bales of goods and lay hold of the merchants as they pass to buy . . . and I hear they are sharp in their dealings, such ranges of piercing eyes and importunate faces and voices I have not seen before. (In Tom Paine Hall, the buyers rush out) when the bell rings, for they are fined if they are found in the place when the bell ceases ringing.

The coal pits being very near to Leeds, the fewel is so cheap as not to be an object. In the lodging houses they include coal as their furniture. Behind the grate and over the fire a heap of coals is deposited for the day. As they are wanted they are drawn down with the poker; it is very convenient, but its appearance in a genteel appartment is not quite so well.

I am much struck with the provision about Leeds for the thirsty horse, the number of large stone cisterns in the road provided for that purpose. The footpath of broad flat stones of an equal size, extended for miles around the town, strike one. Many of them for a mile together are as neat as a London pavement, but without a curb-stone. I am told they last a long time. The whole path up Woodhouse Lane, a mile at least, has not been repaired with ten new stones for fifteen years.

I have mentioned that the common people, especially the women, are agreeable. They seem from the villages round the town all as of one family, the resemblance to each other is so great. Their general character is a round face, rather high cheekbones, fair, thin, healthy cheeks. But the chief description is the hollow beneath the under-lip sinks deeper than usual, and from thence the chin suddenly and strongly advances, and a little turned up, as the cucumber chin, agreeable to vulgar expression. Their eyes rather lively blue, the brows rather determined, not arched, but closer than usual upon the eyes. Certainly they look not like fools, but what may be called cunning . . . In other things the faces of the men, notwithstanding their observing, sharp eyes, do not resemble the countenances of the women. The ladies of Leeds do not in general appear beautiful, but I expect to see very few more virtuous places.

*c.***1800**

The Wensleydale Lad or *Leeds Old Church* was a popular song in Leeds and the surrounding area from the early nineteenth century. It describes the experiences of a naive young dalesman who has come into Leeds to enjoy all the excitements of one of its great fairs, probably that of 8th-9th November, when young people stood around Briggate in order to get themselves hired as servants for the coming year.
Halliday, W. J. & Umpleby A.S. (eds); *The White Rose Garland* (1949) p.19.

The Wensleydale Lad
When I were at home wi' mi father an' mother, I nivver had na fun;
They kept me goin' frae morn to neet, so I thowt frae them I'd run.

Leeds old church was the largest medieval church in West Yorkshire, its nave, aisles and great north transept all having galleries to enable it to house the vst numbers who flocked here to attend its services every Sunday. Regrettably this fine historic structure was totally demolished in 1838. Here we see it in one of Francis Place's early eighteenth-century engravings.

Leeds Fair were coomin' on, an' I thowt I'd have a spree,
So I put on mi sunday cooat, an' went right merrily.

First thing I say were t'factory, I nivver seed one afore;
There were threads an' tapes, an' tapes and' silks, to sell by monny a score.
Owd Ned turn'd iv'ry wheel, and' iv'ry wheel a strap,
'Begor!' says I to t'maister-man, 'Owd Ned's a rare strong chap.'

Next I went to Leeds Owd Church-I were nivver i' one i' mi days,
An' I were maistly ashamed o' misel, for I didn't knaw their ways;
There were thirty or forty folk, i' tubs an' boxes sat,
When up cooms a saucy owd fellow. Says he, 'Noo, lad, tak off thi hat'.

Then in there cooms a great Lord Mayor, an' over his shooders a club,
An' he gat into a white sack-poke, an' gat into t' topmost tub.
An' then there cooms anither chap, I thinks they called him Ned,
An' he gat into t'bottommost tub, an' mocked all t'other chap said.

An' then I heard a shufflin' row, I couldn't mak what aboot,
An' chap donn'd up i't'white sack-poke, began a-shootin' oot,

Tellin' o't'rich folk's road to Heaven, an't'poor folk's road to Hell.
Thowt I to misel, tha silly owd fooil, tho doesn't knaw t'road thisel.

So they began to preach an' pray, they prayed for George, oor King;
When up jumps t'chap i' t'bottommost tub. Says he, 'Good folks, let's sing'.
I thowt some sang varra weel, while other did grunt an' groan,
Ivvery man sang just what he wad, so I sang 'Darby an' Joan'.

When preachin' an' prayin' were over, an' folks wer gangin' away,
I went to t'chap i' t'topmost tub. Says I, 'Lad, what's to pay?'
'Why, nowt' says he, 'my lad'. Begor! I were right fain.
So I clicked hod o' mi gret club stick, an' went whistlin' oot again.

1802

Richard Warner, (1763-1857) entered the church in 1790, about which time he commenced a voluminous series of topographical and antiquarian works. Many of these concerned the south-western counties, but this account comes from his tour of the northern counties.

Cheapside was one of the six 'streets' which surrounded the central courtyard of the Coloured Cloth Hall. In this illustration from George Walker's Costume of Yorkshire *of 1814 the weavers stand behind their pieces of coloured woollen cloth, while the merchants pass amongst them, examining the wares, and offering appropriate prices in barely audible whispers.*

Warner, R. *A Tour Through the Northern Counties of England and the Borders of Scotland* (1802), I, pp.237-40.

Leeds, . . .a town rising to first importance in point of internal commerce; chiefly owing to its advantageous centrical situation, and partly to the spirit of the inhabitants, which, however, may be considered as much an effect as a cause. Several instances were pointed out to us of successful industry, in persons who from journeymen had arisen to princely independence; a proof at once of the profits and extend of the cloth trade in these parts. The advantages which have resulted to the town of Leeds in particular from this branch of English manufactures, may be readily imagined from the increase it has experienced in population within these twenty-five years. This, in 1775, amounted to seventeen thousand one hundred and seventeen; and in 1800, to thirty thousand, exclusive of ten thousand in the two adjoining parishes.

The most curious feature of this place is its markets for mixed and white cloths, which are held every Tuesday and Saturday for the former, and every Saturday for the latter, in large halls erected for the purpose: the one for mixed cloths, a quadrangular building one hundred and twenty-seven yards and half long and sixty-six broad; the other of the same form, but different dimensions, ninety-nine yards long and seventy broad. Here the cloths are exposed for sale in their rough state, as they are delivered from the fulling-mill. The merchants, who are the purchasers, have them dressed, dyed, and pressed, for the retail dealers.

The progress of good sense, and gradual growth of notions of utility, within this last century, are marked by the successive improvements which have taken place in the mode of selling this valuable article.

One hundred and twenty years ago the mixed cloths were exposed for sale upon the unsheltered battlements of the Aire bridge, open to all the inclemency of the weather, and all the dirt and injuries of passing carriages. It required nearly fifty years to convince the factors of the absurdity of this system, when the matter was but little mended by carrying the article into Brigge-Street, and offering it to the merchant, spread on temporary stalls. In 1758, however, the trade had acquired wisdom enough to reform their plan altogether; the mixed cloth hall was built at the expence of the manufacturers; and about seventeen years afterward, another for the white cloths upon a similar plan.

Nothing can be more judicious, convenient, or systematic, than the arrangement of the wares, and the regulations of the sellers, in these receptacles. The larger or mixed cloth hall is laid out into six aisles, each containing two rows of stalls, amounting in all to one thousand seven hundred and seventy; every one of which is twenty-two inches in front, and is the freehold property of the manufacturer who occupies it, who can transfer it to any other manufacturer, (at a premium of about £16) provided he had served a regular apprentice-ship to the making of mixed cloth; without which service no one can be admitted. The white cloth hall contains one thousand two hundred and ten stands, upon the same plan as the other. The hour of sale in the mixed cloth hall is from half-past eight to half-past nine; in the white cloth ditto from a quarter before ten to a quarter before eleven.

But exclusive of the cloth trade, Leeds is brought upon a par with our first commerical towns by several other considerable manufactories. One for the making of sail-cloth employs nearly eighteen hundred people. The Cotton-mill, belonging to Messrs. Coupland, Wilkinson and Coupland, is a concern of great extent; its grand and complicated operations, carried on by the power of one vast steam-engine, built by Mr Murray, of Leeds, performing the work of forty horses, by machinery as beautiful and neat as that of a watch. Potteries and carpet manufactories also contribute to increase the riches of the town, whose advantages are rendered incalculable by rivers and canals, and inexhaustible mines of admirable coals on every side.

1802

C.Dibdin *Observations on a Tour* vol 2 (1802) 266

"From Harrogate I proceeded to Leeds on the twenty-fourth. This astonishingly busy and opulent place continued to have all the bustle in which I had been formerly accustomed to see it: but it seemed to have lost much of that fine generous freedom for which I had then admired it. This was so evident that I could not avoid noticing it, and in consequence found that the prodigious number of Quakers, and other sectaries, which have within a few years settled there, have completely altered the complection of the place. It is, however, perhaps much richer than ever. Leeds has been, according to the lovers of antiquity, a variety of things. It has been a village, a farm worth seven pounds four shillings; it has been a wood in a town and a town in a wood. It is now, however, what I have described it, and will no doubt long continue one of the seats of industry and opulence by which this commercial nation is so nobly distinguished.

1806

Report from the committee on the woollen manufacture of England (1806) p.444-5.
Jovis, 5⁰ die Junii 1806.
JAMES GRAHAM, Esquire (A Member of the Committee) Examined by the Committee.
Are you acquainted with the part of the West Riding of Yorkshire where the woollen manufacture is carried on? Yes.

Will you have the goodness to state the result of your observations and experience, so far as they may throw a light upon the subjects under consideration in this committee? — I became connected with the county of York so long ago as the year 1782, and possessed of a small property in the neighbourhood of Leeds, let out at that time in agricultural farms; I continued it from that time without making any enquiry into the general situation or nature of the trade of that country, and let them upon the same terms for fourteen years, the leases expired in 1795; previous to that, in 1794 and 1795, being in the habit of visiting manufacturers and merchants, particularly an uncle of Mrs. Graham's, Mr Edmund Lodge, they suggested to me that it would be most beneficial thing to the country to divide those agricultural farms into small allotments for clothiers, not only to myself as proprietor but to the country at large, that they thought it would encrease the domestic system, and encourage it very much; Mr Lodge being the possessor of an estate called Eccleshill, in the neighbourhood, was proceeding on the same plan. I visited from that time almost every clothmaker's house in the neighbourhood, to discover the best plan of building, and soon after I began and built twelve or fourteen houses in the neighbourhood, every one of which was immediately taken at almost any price I chose to fix, with five, six, seven, eight or ten acres of land, according to the ability of the man; in Armley, Bramley, Horseforth, and the neighbouring places, from 1795 to 1796 to the present time, it will undertake

to say, having visited twice a year, during that time, every part of that country, not only the population is encreased but the domestic manufacturers have encreased in number as well as in wealth, if one may judge from appearances; they are now, instead of living shut up in narrow streets, in towns extending themselves into the middle of a field; you may see two or three manufacturers houses in almost every field in Armley; they are doubled within these ten years in Bramley, nearly the same in Horseforth; they have encreased very greatly, not perhaps in the same proportion, in Kirkstall and Headingly, there are not a single manufacturer when I first went, now there are at least fifteen or twenty master manufacturers; this continued five or six years; I made enquiry of every merchant, I found that they were raising a cry against factories; I had several deputations from the Cloth Halls; I made enquiry into their supposed apprehensions that the Factories would destroy the domstic system, and, after every enquiry and mature deliberation and consideration, I was satisfied that, so far from injuring them, it must be of very great benefit, and on that ground alone I was applied to by some Merchants at Leeds, to build a manufactory to let out, in order to promote the domestic system; I built a manufactory, and let it to a great manufacturer, and I am sure since it has been built it does not benefit the letting the land, but it incites the domestic manufacturer to a competition; this I found on the enquiries I made, and the examinations of various parts. I have seen myself that the improvements in the factory are very great indeed, there are a variety of cloths made which could not be attempted by domestic clothiers, dyeing, for instance, they could not carry to the extent in the domestic system they do in the factory; Mr Gott has introduced into Yorkshire a most advantageous scheme of dyeing by steam instead of water, which has cost him many thousand pounds in the experiments he has made; great improvements have been like-wise in dyeing blues, scarlets, and blacks; for some time Mr Gott expended very large sums of money in his experiments, which no man but a great capitalist could have done; they will produce a great saving of expence; but there are also other advantages from the Factories, they are continually trying experiments and making improvements, the great improvements in machinery arise from the great capitalists; on that ground I certainly did encourage a factory about five years ago; and I have found that the domestic manufactory and the factory system are encreasing each other, and are carried on to much great advantage where there are factories than where there are solely domestic manufacturers. If the factory system were to exclude from the country the domestic system it would be dreadful indeed, for it is very pleasing in Yorkshire to see the domestic clothiers living in a field, with their homestead, rather than shut up in a street. The encrease of population has been very great, I dare say the Merchants have encreased double; I can remember the time when there were not seven carriages kept in Leeds, and now I dare say there are a hundred; and I think the domestic clothiers have nearly doubled in the district to which I speak, between Bradford and Leeds, and up to Wakefield; I can state the names almost of the persons possessed of property, and freeholders in Armley, who are doubled within these ten years; I think they are nearly doubled in Bramley, another township, and I dare say they are trebled in some parts, therefore I think that the apprehensions, as I have often said to the Trustees of the Cloth Halls, of themselves and others of the domestic manufactures, are not well sounded; if they were to lose any labour by the introduction of machinery, I should be happy to satisfy them, by giving up to them the property I have there.

Do the Committee understand you right, that the interest you have in the success of the factory system, in consequence of your having built one factory, is as nothing compared with the interest you have in the preservation and prosperity of the domestic system? — Certainly.

Examined by Mr Harrison.

Has the encrease in Armley been taken, with reference to the statement delivered in by Mr Ellis, subsequent to its being doubted whether he had given a correct statement? — Yes; and I can give in the name of every person who has been a domestic Clothier.

It appeared by that, that there had been a considerable decrease? — Yes, but it is not correct by any means; I have in my hand a statement of the names of the persons seven years ago, and now I have received this information, which has been collected by some of the most respectable men in Armley, and from my own knowledge of the place, I believe, it to be correct; in 1786 eighty master Clothiers, in 1791 ninety-five, in 1796 one hundred and ten, in 1801 one hundred and thirty; at this present time there are one hundred and sixty master Clotheirs in Armley, the names of whom, if it is necessary, I will deliver in.

1806

John Ryley (1747-1815) was master of Leeds Charity School and a prominent mathematician. Editor of *The Leeds Correspondent* and compiler of two directories of Leeds, his two guides to Leeds

of 1806 and 1808 give masterly descriptions of the elegant building developments in the Georgian west end of the town.
Ryley, J. *The Leeds Guide* (Leeds 1806) pp.66-74.

Perhaps the most pleasing view of Leeds is from the rising ground on the road to Beeston, from which the elegant buildings of Park-Row, Park-Place, the Cloth-Hall, the Infirmary, and the different churches, may be seen to great advantage.

The greatest length of the town is from West to East, and which taken from Park-Place the western extremity, to its eastern termination, St Peter's Square, is about one mile and a half; from North to South it does not extend more than half a mile. In this estimate several streets and squares not joined to the town by a continuity of buildings are omitted.

We shall begin our present survey at the west end of the town, where the object that first solicits attention is Park-Place, which is a very elegant range of buildings, with a South-aspect, and which commands a very pleasing view of the country, particularly of the river Aire; all the houses are built in a very superior style, and, are principally inhabited by affluent merchants or gentlemen who have retired from business. The promenade in Park-Place is, without exception, one of the most pleasing in the town. Immediately to the North of Park-Place is the New Road to Bradford, which was first opened for carriages in the year 1802; this road, besides avoiding much hilly ground saves at least half a mile, in the distance from Leeds to Kirkstall, (three miles) where it terminates, and to which place a broad flagged foot path is continued, to the great comfort of pedestrians, who here

All the road traffic entering Leeds from London and the south passed over the medieval Leeds Bridge, which had to be widened in 1730, 1760 and 1796 in order to cope with the increasing trade. William Harvey's drawing of 1849 shows both the heavy waggons passing over it, and the barges squeezing between its narrow arches, while a local 'logger' propels himself through while balancing precariously on huge balks of timber. This bridge remained in use up to 1871-3, when it was replaced by the present elegant cast-iron structure.

perambulate in great numbers, particularly on Sundays, when the road is crowded with well dressed people.

On the north side of the New Road is, St Paul's Square and though the houses are not equal to those in Park-Place, they are all well-built in the modern style. On the south side of this Square stands St Paul's Church, a very elegant structure in the modern style of architecture. The area of the Square is laid out with considerable taste, and in a few years will furnish a very agreeable promenade. Following the line of the New Road we arrive at the Infirmary, which, with the Mixed Cloth-Hall form one side of a very extensive square, but which from being built at very different periods, has no aggregate name. The West side is called east-parade, the North, south-parade, and the East, park-row; the whole of which consists of genteel, well-built houses; the area of the square, which is very extensive, is partly laid out in gardens and partly used as tenter ground.

Passing on a short but crooked, narrow and ill-built street called Swine-Gate we arrive at the River Aire, over which a strong and well-built Bridge, of four circular arches; it is uncertain in what year it was erected, but it must have been some years after the reign of James I, as in a survey published in his reign there was a Ferry where the Bridge now stands, the profits of which formed part of the jointure of his consort Queen Ann. The Ferry-House was where the Golden Lion Inn is now situated.

The Bridge was considerably widened a few years since, and an additional foot-path erected on the West side. It is situated at the bottom of a very broad and spacious street, which before the erection of the Bridge appears to have been called Broad-Street, but since has received the appellation of Bridge-Gate, or as it is corruptly called Briggate, which is a very nobel and spacious street; and from the foot of the Bridge to Moot-Hall is about four hundred and fifty yards. If the row of houses which is built in the middle of the street, dividing it for the distance of one hundred and twenty yards into two miserable streets, we had almost said alleys, should ever be removed, this street would probably be equalled by few out of London, as the distance from the Bridge to the Head-Row, is near half a mile. The street formed on the East side of Moot-Hall, is the Shambles, the West side is called Back of the Shambles; that part of the street which is above this nuisance, is the Corn-Market, where a convenient Cross is erected, from which it receives the name of Cross-Parish; and is not only the market for corn, but also for butter, eggs and poultry. At the top of Cross-Parish is a narrow street generally called new-street, which leads to St John's church, which may be considered as the present northern boundary of the town. The corner house on the west side of the street is of great antiquity, and was formerly the chantry of St Mary Magdalen, founded by Wm Evers, Vicar of Leeds, Anno 1470.

We mentioned the Head Row as terminating Cross-Parish; this street has since the building of New-Street, been divided into Upper and Lowerhead-Row. Upperhead-Row is to the West of Cross Parish, and has hitherto had more of antiquity in it than any street in the town, but during the writing of this, many of the old buildings on the South side of it have been taken down, and new houses are erecting in their room. Pursuing our walk up the street, we pass a narrow lane or street called Land's-Lane, which from its situation is very capable of being converted into an elegant and airy street.

Passing the Old Bar to Burley we arrive at a new well-built street called Albion-Street, and which is perhaps the pleasantest in the town; at the upper end of it on the West side is erected the new Methodist Meeting, which is a very neat and elegant structure; the houses in this street are remarkably well built, and are chiefly inhabited by professional gentlemen and persons in a wholesale line of business, as no retail shops are allowed to be opened in it; on the West side of the street is situated the Concert Room, under which is a small Cloth-Hall. A road by the side of this building leads to Albion Chapel. On the east side of Albion Street some elegant houses have lately been erected, which are to form part of a street that is to open into Briggate, (Commercial Street) near the Moot-Hall; this, when accomplished, will be one of the greatest improvements which have ever taken place in the town, as, independent of its other advantages, it will introduce a current of air, where it is much wanted into the very heart of the town. Continuing our ramble down Albion Street, we enter Bore, or as it is now generally written Boar-Lane. This street was formerly the road from the castle to the town, and tho' narrow in some places, contains several very good houses, especially a stately mansion fronted with wrought stone, and to which the New Bank is now attached. Immediately adjoining this building is Trinity Church, it is to be lamented that the buildings on the East side of it render it impossible to see it to any advantage; were these houses removed, and the entrance into Briggate widened to a line with this church, it would be an inconceivable improvement to the appearance of the town, and render this church one of its greatest ornaments.

Leedes possesses the capabilities of becoming perhaps one of the handsomest towns in the kingdom, if they were judiciously improved. It is devoutly to be wished that another Mr Harrison would arise, who would devote his talents and opulence to the improvements of it. Boar-Lane opens into Briggate, opposite a short new street called Duncan-Street, which consists of new well built houses, and is used as a flesh-market; there is however, a high dead wall at the North East side of it, that substracts considerably from its general good appearance.

1807

Mrs Siddons (1755-1831) was one of the great figures of the late Georgian theatre. For a period in the 1770s her manager was Tate Wilkinson, and it was in the course of her visits to his seasons at the Leeds Theatre that the following observations were made.
Kennard, A. *Mrs Siddons (1887) The letter was written to Lady Harcourt from the Star and Garter at Kirkstall on 5 July 1807.*

"You see where I am, and must know the place by representations as well as reports, I daresay, at least my lord does, yea, 'every coigne and vantage' of this venerable pile, and envies me the view of it just before me where I am writing. This is an inn. I set myself down here for the advantage of pure air and perfect quiet, rather than lodge in Leeds, most disagreeable town in His Majesty's dominions, God bless him. This day my task finishes. I have played there four nights, and am very tired of Kirkstall Abbey. It is too sombre for a person of my age, and I am no antiquarian. It is, however, extremely beautiful'.
Mattison, A. 'Centenary Account of Mrs Siddons visit to Yorkshire 1789' *Yorkshire Evening Post* (June 1931).

"From York the company came to Leeds, when Mrs Siddons opened the season on 1 June with the play of "Jane Shore". On the four succeeding nights she appeared in the characters of Queen Mary, Calistra, Dianora, and Lady Macbeth.

When, as Lady Macbeth, she was playing the sleep-walking

scene, a boy who had been sent out by someone in the company for some porter, stupidity marched, jug in hand, on the stage, despite many attempts to stop him, to the great amusement of the audience, and the equally great irritation of the actress. Her annoyance was still further increased when, later on, as she was taking the poison, a rough occupant in the "gods" bawled out "soop it up, lass". These unpleasant incidents the tragedienne could not forgive, and when the curtain fell down she exclaimed, as she stood behind it: "Farewell, ye brutes!"

1810

William Hutton (1723-1815) started life as an apprentice in a Derby silk-mill, but by a variety of means he became a well-to-do figure in the public life of Birmingham. His main interests were in local history and topography, subjects on which he produced a large number of well-researched volumes.
Hutton, W. *A Trip to Coatham* (1810) 33.

Leeds is rising, and will continue to rise, except checked by a *just and necessary war*. The river, having been made navigable, gives an easy access to the markets. The number of elegant buildings recently erected, shews what they have been able to accomplish; but the enterprising spirit of the inhabitants will perform future wonders. Good fortune stamps the place her own.

The returns on the market-day at their Cloth-halls are wonderful.

The prosperity of a place may, in some measure, be ascertained by the value of land in its vicinity. A gentleman who resides at Hounslet, the village adjoining to Leeds, told us that he had, at various times, purchased twenty-two acres of land, now in a ring-fance, which, upon the average, cost him three-hundred pounds *per* acre. Upon the back part of this land he had erected his house, works, &c. He had no doubt, were he inclined, but he could dispose of the front land at a thousand pounds an acre.

Another gentleman told us he had erected a steam-engine, and extensive machinery for scribbling, shearing, dying, &c. upon a lease for the short space of twenty-one years.

A third gentleman remarked to us, that he had recently agreed for the purchase of a small piece of land, at a most extravagant price; he did not say what. But, as he could not make one bargain without making two, he applied to the Lord of the Manor for permission to use a small brook which ran by the side of the intended purchase, and of which the lord made no use. That he had offered a thousand pounds, which the lord was then in doubt whether he should accept. Water seems as dear as land.

The inhabitants are extremely prudent in regulating their cloth-markets, so as to prevent deception.

1810-11

Louis Simond (1767-1831) was a native of Lyon. In the early nineteenth century he journeyed throughout England, Switzerland, Italy and Sicily, then recording his experiences in a series of books published in Paris between 1810 and 1828. This extract comes from his *Voyage d'un Francais en Angleterre* of 1810-11.
Simond, L. *Journal of a Tour & Residence in Great Britain* (Edinburgh 1815).

The meadows are of the most vivid green, and the trees are budding, much as about New York a month later; the weather

so fine and mild as to travel with the glasses down. Stage-coaches pass us continually with their absurd lading of passengers on the top, — twelve or fifteen nodding heads. The night had closed when we approached Leeds, and from a height, north of the town, we saw a multitude of fires issuing, no doubt from furnaces, and constellations of illuminated windows (manufactories) spread over the dark plain. We soon reached streets of good-looking shops, and stopped at the door of the inn, — a large bustling one, always less comfortable than those of lesser towns.

March 13 — After breakfast a lady (Mrs R.) for whose nephew we had a letter, called on us in his absence, and offered very obligingly to show us, the lions of the place, which she did with equal good nature and intelligence.

The clothiers' hall is a vast quadrangular fireproof building round a court-yard; it is the joint property and warehouse of 2000 private manufacturers, half-farmers, who have only a loom or two kept going at leisure times. Twice-a-week, for one hour, they appear each at his stand, two and a half feet wide, and perhaps ten feet deep, with their stock piled up behind them, and samples in their hands. These stands are arranged on each side of a long gallery, with a passage between.

The merchants walk along the double line comparing their orders with the samples, and making purchases, generally at a uniform price. There is a great deal of business done in a very short time, and with very few words, *although* many of the stands are occupied by women, as our conductress informed us. This is a respectable set of people, and a pleasing instance of domestic manufactures, so preferable to the crowds and depravity of great establishments. Cloth has lately fallen in price from 35 to 25 shillings, in consequence of the increasing obstructions to the British trade.

The men, whose business is the combing and shearing the cloth, work by the piece, and earn 5s a day, by working from four in the morning to eight at night. They are described as very extravagant and very poor; brutified, vicious, and troublesome to their employers. They see, with an evil eye, a machine about to be set up, to do this work by the steam-engine, and disturbances are apprehended. We have observed the mark of *Jounaux freres, de Sedan*, on pieces of broad-cloth destined for the continent.

The hospital, or infirmary, is remarkable for the good order and cleanliness of its interior; the patients are placed in rooms, not wards, from four to eight in each. The only improvement the philanthropic Howard, visiting this hospital, could suggest, was, that there ought to be a sufficient number of apartments for some of them in rotation, to remain unoccupied for some weeks, which was done accordingly.

This town has doubled in the last twenty years, therefore a great part of the buildings are modern and comfortable, with gardens, planted squares, and flowers in every window. We were shown a good library and reading-room; the librarian is a lady.

1819

John Bigland (1750-1832) was a Yorkshire village schoolmaster who became a successful professional author in his fifties, and wrote twenty books in the last thirty years of his life.
Bigland, J. *The Beauties of England and Wales* (Yorkshire 1819) 775-796.

The town of Leeds is generally well built, almost entirely of brick; but its different quarters form, one with another, a striking contrast. In the eastern parts, on the banks of

(Sheepscar Beck), the houses are mean, and the streets and lanes dirty, crooked and irregular, emitting disagreeable smells from the dying houses and different manufacturers, while the discoloured and dirty torrent puts a person in mind of the waters of Styx and Cocytus . . .

The southern edge of the town, along the banks of the Aire, is almost equally disagreeble; and although containing some good houses, has, in great measure, the appearance of a prison. But the middle and western parts display several fine streets and elegant new buildings. The breadth of the town, from north to south, is not much above half a mile; but it extends not less than a mile and a half in length, from east to west. It is divided nearly into two equal parts by Briggate and the market place, which open into each other, running nearly in a line from south to north. Briggate, the principal street in Leeds, is about 500 yards in length and above 30 yards in breadth; in this street the cloth market was formerly held on Tuesdays and Saturdays at an early hour in the morning. At the upper end of Briggate is the Moot-hall, the front of which is stone, supported by columns and arches, with the arms of the town "in relievo" between two maces, the ensigns of mayorality . . .In a niche over the arms of the town, is a statue of Queen Anne in white marble, by Carpenter, the gift of Alderman Milner.

From the Moot-hall to the market place, the street is divided, by a row of buildings, into two narrow streets, or passages; that to the east is the shambles, the other, on the west side, is called the back of the shambles. The market-place, or, as it is usually called, Cross-Parish, is a very spacious street, with a large market-cross near the south end. At the top of the market-place is the head-row, so called from its elevated situation, as it rises, with an easy ascent, to the crown of the hill, on the southern declevity of which the town is situated . . .

In the middle of the town, both to the east and west of Briggate, and the market-place, are several good streets, and many large and handsome houses. But the western part displays the greatest degree of elegance. In this quarter is a spacious square environed with handsome brick houses, which being built at different times, has no general name. The east side is called Park-Row, the western in denominated East-parade, the north is distinguished by the name of South Parade; the south side is formed by the Mixed Cloth Hall, and the General Infirmary. The centre is partly laid out in gardens, but the larger proportion is used as tenter ground. Park Square is also composed of elegant modern houses; and the centre is laid out in walks, and planted with shrubs. On the south side of this square is St Paul's church, a very handsome structure of stone, and quite modern; having been opened for divine service on Christmas Day, in the year 1794. To the south of Park Square, and separated from it by the New Road to Kirkstall, is Park Place, a row of very handsome houses, fronting towards the south, and commanding a fine view of the river Aire and the neighbouring hills . . .

The corn market is held every Tuesday in Cross-parish. The shambles display great abundance of butcher's meat; and the beef is remarkably fine. On Saturday evening the town is always crowded with the working people of the neighbouring villages, who come to lay in a stock of provisions for the ensuing week. The fish-markets are held on Monday and Thursday. The quantity of fruit and garden stuff sold every market day, especially on Tuesday, is astonishing. A considerable quantity of these articles is brought from Pontefract, and a great deal being purchased in Leeds market by hucksters, is carried to be disposed of at Bradford and Halifax. The markets, indeed, are almost wholly supplied from the agricultural district to the east-ward. The whole country, from Leeds to Lancashire, does to produce corn sufficient to supply one-sixth part of the inhabitants. Besides the weekly markets, here are two annual fairs, each of which continues two days, viz. July 10th and 11th, for horses and pedlary wares, and November 8th and 9th, chiefly for horned cattle.

The chief manufacture of the town and its vicinity is cloth, which was formerly almost wholly of the coarser kinds; but the manufacture of superfines has of late greatly increased, as has also that of swansdowns, toilenets, kersymeres, and various other fancy articles. Several manufactures of sacking, canvas, linen, and thread have been established and carried on to a very considerable extent. Here are also carpet manufactories, and a number of cotton mills, most of which are worked by means of steam engines. In the neighbourhood are likewise a considerable manufactory of the finer sorts of earthern-ware, and several founderies. On the banks of the Aire, and on the streams which empty themselves into that river, are numerous mills for grinding corn, dyer's-wood, rape-seed, etc.

But although Leeds has long been distinguished as one of the first manufacturing towns, its opulence is still derived from commerce.

It is the principal mart of the woollen manufactures in the west riding, and a great part of the cloths etc. pass through the hands of merchants of Leeds . . .The town of Leeds possesses numerous and important advantages as an emporium of inland trade; seated on the edge of one of the chief manufacturing districts of England, it is abundantly supplied with various articles of merchandise; while the navigable river Aire, with the Leeds and Liverpool canal, affords an easy communication with both the eastern and western seas.

The environs of Leeds are pleasant and beautiful. The vale of the Aire, extending both eastward and westward to a great distance, is one of the finest features of the country, and the soil is extremely fertile. Within three or four miles to the south of the town, is abundance of coal; and to the cheapness of that indispensable article may be attributed and flourishing state of the manufacturers. Within a mile of the town, towards the north-west, are vast quarries of an argillaceous schist, which supply the neighbourhood and country down the river with flag stones. Some of the higher parts of the parish of Leeds are rocky and barren; but in the valleys, and on the declevities, the land is extremly rich, and, by reason of the great plenty of manure, and the populousness of the country, is in a high state of cultivation.

1820

Yorkshire Weekly Post 1 August 1908 p.15
(originally in *London Magazine*, Nov.1820. 'T' may have been William Hazlitt).

Oh! Smoked city! Dull and dirty Leeds!
Thou mayst be well for trade, and eke for wealth,
And thou mayst cleanse thyself, at times — by stealth,
Like men who do, but never own, good deeds;
And thou mayst be a place where commerce feeds
Hundreds of hungry mouths, both girls and boys;
And thous mayst show how spinning thread hath joys
Beyond the vicious pleasures Idlenesse breeds.
Of Leeds I this deny not; but if e'er
Again, at any hour of morn, noon, night,
My soul or body be caught lingering there,
Unless hard driven for cash, or else by fright,
May I nee'er kiss my lady's red lip bright!
This, by her beauty and my hopes, I swear.

Child labour helped to boost the success of the first generation of wool textile factories in Leeds, even though eminent local surgeons such as William Hey considered that, when pursued too far, it stunted the growth, debilitated the constitution, and led to severe accidents. These factory children in George Walker's Costume of Yorkshire *of 1814 wear their typical mill smocks, carry their daily food in small round baskets, and have the dark blue complexion which frequently resulted from their work.*

1822

Leeds Intelligencer, Mon-February 11 1822.

On Saturday Week, Geo. Dyson, a boy about 13 years of age, while employed in filling a carding machine at Armley Mill, unfortunately got entangled in the machinery, by which accident his thigh was severed from his body, and he was in other respects so dreadfully injured as to occasion his death shortly afterwards.

Yewdall, J. *The Toll Bar and Other Poems* (1827) p.65.

LINES
ON THE DEATH OF GEORGE DYSON, WHO WAS KILLED
AT ARMLEY MILL, FEB.2. 1822.

Ah! what is man? a reed, a worm,
As weak, as helpless, and infirm,
His days are few, his moments fly,
He's born to live, and doom'd to die.

His life's a span, a thought, a breath,
This hour in health, the next in death;
From earth he came, and soon he must,
Return again to mother dust.

This very morn, (as I've just read)
A brother liv'd, that's now laid dead.
Liv'd! did I say? — Yes, liv'd and well,
As many witnesses can tell.

His health as usual, unimpar'd,
He rose, he dress'd, no danger fear'd,
Went to his work this morning soon,
But was a corpse — before 'twas noon.

1828

Herman Ludwig Heinrich Furst von Puckler — Muskau (1785-1871) German nobleman, writer and traveller, inherited the large estate of Muskau, which he redesigned according to the tenets of landscape gardening he had absorbed and admired in England. He wrote extensively and wittily on his travels in Europe, North Africa and the Near East, and his writings reflect the manners and morals of the peoples he visited.

von Puckler, Muskau Prince H.L.H. *Tour in Germany, Holland & England 1826, 1827 and 1828.*
(1832) vol IV p.210

Oct. 1st

I reached the manufacturing town of Leeds just in the twilight. A transparent cloud of smoke was diffused over the whole space which it occupies, on and between several hills, a hundred red fires shot upwards into the sky and as many towering chimneys poured forth columns of black smoke.

The huge manufactories, five stories high, in which every window was illuminated, had a grand striking effect. Here the toiling artisan labours far into the night, and that same romantic features might not be wanting in the whirl of business and illumination of industry two ancient gothic churches reared their heads above the mass of houses and the moon poured her silver light upon their towers, and seemed to damp the hard glare of the busy crowd below, with serene majesty.

Oct. 2nd

First I visited the Market Hall, a beautiful building, in which the market is held under a glass roof; then the Cloth Hall, an immense room entirely filled with cloth of all sorts and colours, and lastly, the largest cloth manufactory of the place, which is worked by three steam engines. Here you begin with the raw material (the sorting of the wool), and finish with the perfect cloth; so that if you took a tailor with you you might bring your wool into the manufactory in the morning and come out with a coat made of it in the evening. Our friend R-actually performed this feat, and wore the coat for a very long time, with great predilection. The various machines are ingenious in the highest degree; but the stench and the wholesome air, as well as the dust in many operations, msut be very unhealthy to the poor workmen, who moreover were all of a dark blue colour. The young man who showed us the manufactory, said, however, that the cotton manufactories were much more unhealthy, from the fine and subtle dust, that in them a workman seldom reached his fiftieth year, whereas here there were instances of men of sixty. The gothic churches which yesterday produced such an effect at a distance, presented nothing remarkable on a nearer inspection, and the town itself, enveloped in an everlasting fog produced by the smoke, which never ceases day or night, is the most disagreeable place you can imagine.

1830

William Cobbett (1763-1835) was a prolific writer, pamphleteer, and Radical politician. After service in the army in Canada, he became a Tory propagandist, but then, in 1804, he joined the radical cause. Most of his books are on political and agricultural subjects, the most famous of these being his *Rural Rides*.
Cobbett, W. *Rural Rides (version edited by G.D.H. & Margaret Cole, vol.II, 1930) pp.604 & 606-7.*

On the 20th (of January 1830) I came on to Leeds; and, after having stopped a litlte while to speak with my friend Mr Foster, of the *Patriot* newspaper; my old and firm friend, Mr Mann, the bookseller; Mr Heaps, and some other friends, we proceeded on to Sir William Ingilby's, at Ripley Castle, which very beautiful place, and still more beautiful village . . .

I have just returned from the theatre in this fine and opulent town (of Leeds), which may be called the London of Yorkshire, and in which I have been received with an enthusiasm which I should in vain endeavour to describe. Here, as in all other places, there prevails *theatrical distress* to an exceeding degree; but I have filled, and over-filled, the whole house, pit, boxes and galleries . . .

On the 26 (of January, 1830) I gave my third lecture at Leeds. I should in vain endeavour to give an adequate description of the pleasure which I felt at my reception, and at the effect which I produced in that fine and opulent capital of this great county of York; for the *capital* it is in fact, though not in name. On the first evening, the play-house, which is pretty spacious, was not completely filled in all its parts; but on the second and the third, it was filled brim full, boxes, pit and gallery; besides a dozen or two of gentlemen who were accommodated with seats on the stage. Owing to a cold which I took at Huddersfield, and which I spoke of before, I was, as the players call it, not in a very good *voice*; but the audience made allowance for that, and very wisely preferred sense to sound. I never was more delighted than with my audience at Leeds; and what I set the highest value on, is, that I produced a prodigious effect in that important town . . .

I cannot quit the subject of Leeds, without acknowledging the friendly attentions that I received from many gentlemen there, particularly from Mr Foster, of that excellent provincial

paper, the "Leeds Patriot"; from Mr Heaps, Mr Mann, and Dr Metcalfe. Here too, I had the pleasure to see for the first time, that Mr Dickenson, who detected the spy, Oliver, and thereby saved, perhaps, scores of the lives of his countrymen; a merit, however, which was claimed by the great *Liar of the North*, commonly so called, who has been fattening for ten years upon the reputation of having performed this great service to Yorkshire. This great *Liar of the North* hid his head while I was in the town, came sneaking to the playhouse, wrapped up in a sort of disguise; but I dare say he will break loose again in due time.

1832

Ely Hargrove's *History of the Castle, Town and Forest of Knaresborough, with Harrogate and its medical waters'* was first published by the Knaresborough bookseller and publisher in 1775, and went through six editions before the author's death in 1818. The substantially revised seventh edition was published by William Langdale in 1832.
Hargrove, E. *History of Knaresborough (1828) 173.*

There are two fairs held annually at Leeds; one on the 10th and 11th of July, and the other on the 8th and 9th of November. On the last of these days young persons of both sexes attend to hire as servants. There is likewise a fortnight fair for cattle and sheep held in the Vicar's Croft Market; also, a quarterly fair for leather, held in the South Market, which is expected to become one of the first in the kingdom.

1833

The report of the Factories Inquiry Commission into children's employment, precurser of much of the legislation against the exploitation of children in factories, is a vast document containing the testimony of many well-known Leeds men, as well as of the victims of the system. It is a fascinating record not only of life in the factories, but of the attitudes and beliefs of the witnesses. As a sample, the evidence of the doctor, the Hunslet overseer and one employee have been selected.
Factories Inquiry Commission. Second Report . . .as to the employment of children in factories (1833) pp.16, 44-5, 58-9.

WILLIAM HAY examined at Leeds, 28 May 1833, by Dr Loudon.

I am a surgeon, and have practised in Leeds upwards of thirty-nine years. I am a native of the town, and was surgeon to the infirmary for eighteen years. I resigned my situation as surgeon about two years and a half ago. I am of opinion that factory labour, when pursued too far, stunts the growth, and debilitates the constitution generally, so as to render it susceptible of diseases of various kinds. It is my opinion also, that the injuries done to the constitution of this kind of employment may be transmitted to posterity.

During my hospital practice diseases of the spine amongst people employed in factories presented themselves very frequently. The annual number of patients who apply for aid may be about 4,000. Of these, I might have seen individually about 800 every year. I have no documents to refer to as to the number of spine diseases, but they were considerable. Some were the result of pure labour; others were the result of labour on a constitution perhaps congenitally weak, or rendered feeble by bad food and other causes.

Numerous surgical cases have also came under my care during the period I have alluded to, but I have no documents to refer to particularly. Many of these arose from the carelessness of the children, many from the negligence of the masters, and some from the sleepiness of the children themselves, induced by the excessive hours of labour.

The deformities of the limbs appeared to be more frequent than the spinal diseases. What I have particularly remarked has been the falling-in of the arch of the foot, the bending in of the knees, relaxation of the ligaments of the ancles was very frequent, and the bending of the large bones. The heads of the large bones have especially been increased and twisted to a considering extent; and these cases I have found to have come from those mills and factories where long hours have been said to be common.

I have practised midwifery as a part of my profession since the commencement of my practice, but I have not remarked that factory labour has been productive of distorted pelvis in the cases where I have been called to, nor am I aware that embryotomy is more common in Leeds than it is anywhere else. I think it right to state, that my midwifery practice has not been much amongst the poor.

I have never particularly attended to the number of hours that they have worked in the factories, and have not specially noticed the ages of those with distorted limbs, but it has been usually from ten to fifteen.

My opinion as a professional man, is that no child should be admitted into a factory under ten years of age, and that the hours of labour should not exceed ten. I would object to eleven hours; indeed I think ten too many for the labour of a young person from ten to eighteen. Above eighteen, with this restriction with regard to the earlier periods of life, any farther legislation might not be necessary. I see no objection to changes of children.

JOHN YEWDALE

I am perpetual overseer to the township of Hunslet; I have held that situation three years. The population of this township is 12,074 by last census. In the year ending April 1832, our parochial disbursements amounted to 3613l., whereof 1597l was applied to the relief of out-door poor. The principal sources of employment to our population within the township are woollen mills, of which there are five within the township. We have also a few employed in earthenware manufactories and glass works. The whole number of inhabited houses is about 3000, of which 2000 are under 5l, rental; showing that nearly the whole of our population is of the labouring class, many of whom find employment in the adjoining township of Leeds. At the census last taken, we found 717 males above twenty, who came under the description of woollen clothiers; part of these would be employed in the woollen factories, and part weaving at their own house. The number employed in earthenware within our own township was 155 males above the age of twenty; also 75 in glass-making. There are also 193 of the same class employed in the collieries at Middleton and Rothwell; and 126 linen weavers working at home. There are no young persons employed in glass-making; but many, both boys and girls, in the earthenware trade. The largest pottery is Mr Wainwright's, called the Leeds, which I will accompany you to see. There are four potteries, and two glass-houses. Two out of the five woollen mills have been standing, one for seven years, the other for one year. There has also been a pottery standing for a long while — for about two years; also a large forge, which has been standing about three years. I forgot to mention also a large cotton mill, which has been standing about seven years, and has just begun again in part. In consequence of all which, we have a great number of cottages unoccupied at this time;

I should think from 400 to 500. At the time we took the census, two years ago, there were ascended to be 318 unoccupied; and I am quite confident there are as many more now as I have mentioned. One effect of it with which I am peculiarly acquainted is, that one-sixth of the whole amount laid has been deficient in the collection; and another is, that our weekly payments have been much increased from people being out of employment. Our weekly disbursement to out-door paupers is from 33l to 35l. taking an average through the year. The lowest limit occurs in the summer, in July, and is 31l; the highest occurs in winder, and is 39l: so that our fluctuations during different seasons of the year are inconsiderable. They depend more upon the failing or reviving, at certain periods, of our main sources of employment; I may say on the state of trade generally. Looking back to the books of 1824, the average seems to be 18l or 19l per week. Passing to those of the year 1830, it seems to be about 25l. The relief is given weekly at the workhouse, in this room, on application of the paupers to a weekly board, consisting of four overseers, and twelve committee-men, and myself. There are seldom more than four or five present besides myself. I act for the whole township, and make all entries in the books, according to the decision who examine the paupers here. The ordinary number of applications are two hundred; not above forty families. I do occasionally take such an account of the families receiving relief as I have already given you, describing the number, ages, and earning of the different members of the family. That is only when I am directed to enquire into any doubtful case at the houses, and such papers as those are not usually preserved. When application is made, we cast up the earnings of the family, and if we find them to have 2s 6d a head, we do not consider it a case for relief, under ordinary circumstances. If we find them short of that, we make up the whole sum to that amount. (The witness here produced a document, being a description of twenty-three families to whom relief had been lately afforded, of which the following is an abstract:)

	Employed	No.		Unemployed	No.
	(6 and 7)	0		(6 and 7)	5
Between	(7 and 8)	0	Between	(7 and 8)	7
the	(8 and 9)	3	the	(8 and 9)	5
ages of	(9 and 10)	0	ages of	(9 and 10)	6
	(10 and 15)	30		(10 and 15)	4
	Total	33		Total	27

With regard to the age at which we expect the children to be employed, our rule has been, until lately at nine years of age we would give no relief in respect of that child, and accordingly take off the usual allowance of 1s 6d for every such child. That practice continued up to within a year of this time, when we changed the age to ten, in consequence of the masters not choosing to employ them before. I believe they have to thank Mr Sadler for that; I mean the children, to whom I consider it an advantage; the parents, I believe, don't consider it so. Sometimes, when a child is strong, and requires a good deal of support, it is necessary he should work, in order to earn a sufficient subsistence, and very often it will do him no harm; but in many cases the children have been employed in too hard at too tender an age. I do not think that observations applies to the present time, except that some of the mills run still too long. I do not think it will do a child of ten years of age any harm to work twelve hours; I mean from six to six, or from six to seven, if only the mills would stop at that hour. I worked in a mill myself about the age of ten, a woollen cloth mill. We had from six to eight. I was there about three years, when I went apprentice. I don't think it did me a morsel of harm at that time. One of my sisters went about seven to the same mill; stayed four or five years; never hurt her health. I don't know that we were strong children; rather under than above average for that. The parents generally managed to find them employment at the age of ten; generally speaking, the parents are extremely anxious to find them employment, before the age the masters are willing to take them. It does not often happen that the children come back upon our list from being out of employment. Occasionally, however, we admit them again to the allowance of 1s 6d during sickness, or even more. That cannot be said to happen very often; we have had a good deal of it lately during the influenza. On such occasions, the parents themselves apply.

Q. Has it occurred, during the period you have acted, that the parents have complained of their children's health being hurt by the long hours of labour? and to what extent has that complaint been usual? — A. Very rarely indeed; but it may occasionally have been the cause to which they have attributed the illness of the children. Our surgeon generally sees these cases; he gives them a note, and sometimes medicine, without relief; it is rare that any serious illness occurs amongst our paupers. We often make enquiries in to arrangements between the parents and children. We say, How much does so and so bring you? They say, 5s or 4s 6d, the child keeping the rest for clothes. This is very frequent in our township, particularly among the girls. I should say the age at which it occurs is about fifteen and upwards; I should say three parts of the whole above that age make such an arrangement. It depends less upon the age, than upon the time at which they are enabled to do this by the amount of their earnings. They are anxious to do it as soon as they can, and become their own mistresses. Many times they leave, if the parents refuse this arrangement, and go into lodgings. It would be a trifle more they would have to pay for board, lodging, and washing elsewhere; say 5s: I think that would be enough. 1s for lodging and washing, and 4s for the rest.

Q. As to the age, then, at which the girls will be generally enabled to insist upon their independence, what is the result of your experience? A. I should say about sixteen.

Q. Will the same amount enable boys to do the same? A. No; I think boys require more expense in keeping; but at the same time they will earn more than the girls. They are not usually so anxious to set themselves up independent as the girls: I should say they average eighteen nearly before they do it.

Q. What age would they be enabled to do it? A. I should say 6s would be about equivalent to a boy's board and lodging, from fourteen to sixteen years of age. About eighteen they pay as much as 8s a week: they are then earning on an average 11s or 12s a week. At sixteen I should say they would be earning 7s a week. As far as my experience goes about the health of children in employment, I should say those in the flax mills are worst: the cotton mill has not been long enough at work to judge by: the next worst I should say were boys in collieries; the earthenware is next worst; the woollen mill I think the healthiest of all. I have had experience of them.

JOHN DAWSON (sworn)

I was between six and seven when I first began to work in Shaw and Tennant's flax-mill in Leeds as a doffer. That is not very hard work; it is taking off the full bobbins, and putting empty ones on: there was perhaps about half-a-dozen doffers in a room containing about fourteen or sixteen sides. Our regular hours then were about from six to seven: I don't

recollect working over-hours there; but it was the case in every mill almost at that time, and I think in Tennant's too sometimes, but I can't particularly remember. My father was over-looker in the room where I was doffing: it is necessary to beat the doffers sometimes to make them mind their work; but not to beat 'em as some over-lookers do. I have been beaten several times as a doffer: my father has beat me many a time as well as other over-lookers. I don't consider doffing hard work at all, except for the standing, and they have liberty to sit sometimes, when they have got all right. I think I left Tennant's at the same time with my father, about the age of ten: we went to Garside's flax-mill. I can't just say what made us leave: it might be disagreement between my father and the time-keeper, or it might be that work was slack, and we could not get sufficient supply of it at that mill. We have had as little there as five and four days a week. I was quite strong in health when I went to Garside's, except I think there was weakness in my knees at that time, from standing so long when young: I am pretty sure it was so. At Garsides's, being bigger and stronger, I was put to heavier work than at Tennant's: that was bobbin-hugging, or carrying bobbins in a basket, by a strap which passed round the forehead and suspended the basket on the back and loins. It would sometimes be very heavy, particularly with the wet bobbins, which I generally had to carry up stairs to the reelers. I felt myself not strong enough for that work: it gave me a pain in my knees. The regular hours here were from six to seven; but we often had to go from half-past five to eight or half-past eight. We had only forty minutes at dinner; none for breakfast or drinking in the spinning rooms. There would be sometimes two bobbin-huggers in a room, sometimes one; I was the only one in my room, which contained about sixteen sides and about half-a-dozen doffers. I was full young enough to undertake that work: I did not begin with it when I first went to Garside's: I was doffing at first, and was afterwards set to it by the over-looker. I was obliged to do it or go. My father was over-looker at this time in the dry side-room; not where I was hugging bobbins. I stopped at it two or three years: the pain and weakness was growing worse all that time, and deformity evidently coming on: my father and mother both observed it: they did not make an application to the over-looker, or to the master, nor did I myself: I did not think so much about it then as I do now. We both left that place and went to Clayton's: I don't know on what account. My knees were quite bent at that time, as bad as ever they have been: I did not see any doctor about 'em until after we left Clayton's. We staid there between three or four years; until my father died: he was an over-looker there. I was set to spinning and doing jobs; any work that wanted doing. The over-looker's business is not to do any work himself, but to see the hands do their work; occasionally he may lend a hand in putting things right. The hours varied at Clayton's more than any place I was at: it was from five to half-past nine sometimes; that was the worst; the regular time from six to seven; time for dinner only forty minutes; none for breakfast or drinking. My father died at Clayton's.

Q. In consequence of hard work? — A. No; he had not hard work to do; it was the unhealthiness of the rooms: the dust and dirt of the different rooms in which he had been over-looker injured his health so that he died between forty and fifty: my mother thought it was that, and many said so that knew him. It was at Garside's his health first began to fail. I have known people who had been in a flax-mill a long time go away from bad health, and never come back; it is more the fresh hands, however, who are obliged to go away, than the old ones; I don't recollect any who died from it, besides my father. I have known of many accidents happening by the machinery both to young and old: there was one death at Clayton's, of a boy who was caught in an upright shaft by his clothes, and killed. I could mention several other bad accidents happening both from the shafts and the frames. There is a deal of machinery boxed off now that used to be exposed when I went first into factories. I was very anxious when a boy to go to school, and learn reading and writing: went always to the Sunday school when I could; very seldom missed: if I did, it was my mother wanting me to stay at home and look after the younger children; sometimes it would be from the want of good shoes or clothes. I was anxious to go also to a night school: could not go there on account of the late hours: was glad to get to bed as soon as I got home, being so tired. My father used, however, to teach us to read: I could read middling well in the Testament at fourteen years of age; we had little time but on the Sunday. I did not learn writing till after my father's death, and till after I had left the factories. Clayton's was not the last I worked at. I went from there, between fourteen and fifteen, to Colbeck's, a flax-mill, Leeds. Did doffing and jobbing there again. The boys employed in bobbin-hugging used, in my time, to be generally about twelve years of age: I began at ten; they ought to be strong to do it even at twelve. I left Colbeck's because the over-looker strapped me; he was a very severe man: that was the last place. My mother was taken ill, and we were both obliged to go into the workhouse. She got better, and went out, leaving me there: I was there about three years: learned there both reading, writing, and accounts, and was put out to learn my present trade of a tailor. At the time I left the factories my limbs were so bad, and my knees so bent, that I could not walk thirty or forty yards without resting. When at the workhouse I was an out-patient of the Infirmary, under Mr Chorley, who gave me bandages and strengthening plasters which did me good: I am better now, though I still walk with difficulty; and my knees are bent as you see.

(The witness shows his knees, which are both dreadfully bent inwards and forwards.)

I have no doubt it arose from the hard work which I was put to at Garside's in hugging the bobbins for so many hours together. I don't know what Mr Chorley thought about it. I was straight as a loich before I went to Garside's. I have not been able to support myself by my trade altogether, without relief from the parish; partly in consequence of my eyesight being so bad: I am obliged to wear glasses at my work. I have been told that cause of working in the factories: I would not say that myself, but I think it was very likely from going so young. It is not a common effect of working in the flax-mills; but the dust does get into the eyes a good deal. I remember being short-sighted very young; when I was ten or eleven years of age. I have known girls very often, after leaving the factories, turn out common prostitutes. Some of them I have known turned away for misbehaving themselves while there: I judge from that they learn bad habits while in the factories. If any of them are found out to be bad characters it is usual to turn them away. From this practice I don't think it does happen that many in the factories are established bad characters: what I mean to say is, that I think they often learn such bad habits in the factories as make them turn out bad after they leave. In the spinning rooms, where I have been as a doffer, the girls are not allowed at all by the master to talk to one another; I have known them fined for that; that is general in all mills, I believe.

Q. How is it they form their bad habits; — A. I don't know how it is; they are wild and giddy; they're bad enough sometimes before they come; they soon show it; many of 'em behave very indecent both among themselves and with the boys, when the over-looker's not there; there are many of them decent and respectable girls; there are often a good many young married women among them. What I am speaking of is principally naughty language that I can remember, when a doffer, to have heard them use to each other: there is a good deal of difference in over-lookers about correcting this. I consider many girls that have gone there decent have been quite the contary when they have left, by seeing the goings on and behaviour of other girls. I have never seen or heard of any bad books, or images, or pictures among them. I have seen, however, representations of that nature done with chalk on the walls of the factories, as well as on paper. I must say, as far as that goes, there is a deal of indecency amongst them. I think I have stated, as near as I can recollect, all I have to say, or wish to say.

1835

Sir George Head (1782-1855) followed an active overseas career in the army, before retiring on half pay in 1823. From that time he concentrated on his writing, for which he had an admirable skill in graphic description. His *Home Tour* brought him into considerable repute as a topographical writer.
Head, Sir G. *A Home Tour through the Manufacturing Districts of England in the summer of 1835* (1835) pp.

In no manufacturing town in England, I imagine is more coal consumed, in proportion to its extent, than Leeds; situated in the heart of a coalfield, and fed by an abundant daily supply, a single glance, whether by day or night, verifies the above conclusion. The sun himself, as by a natural mist, no sooner descends below the horizon, than streams of brilliant gas burst forth from thousands of illuminated windows.

The Old Coal Staithes form one principal point of delivery of the coal brought from the pits, four miles westward, to the town. The entrance to the first of these pits, at Middleton, is by a level on the side of the hill, wherein it is only necessary to enter a few yards in order to see a perfect vein of coal.

The staithes consist of a platform raised upon a row of brick arches, each having an aperture in the summit, so that the cart being brought underneath, in order to receive its load, the coal is at once shot into it from the waggon above . . .

The railroad and locomotive steam-engines are curious and worthy of observation being among the earliest in the country; the latter especially is as different in appearance from the engines in present use, as a state-coach in the days of Queen Anne from any of our modern vehicles. A wheel on one side of the engine works upon a line of cogs, with which the rails on the same side are furnished; thus though by a slow motion, gaining a purchase by rack and pinion. This crazy, rickety old engine continues to grundle along day after day at the rate of about five miles an hour; an extra-ordinary instance, by comparison, of the improvements in machinery of the last fifteen or sixteen years.

Considerable cargoes of coal are brought from the eastern vicinity of the town by the river Aire; of these there are two points of delivery, 'The Crown Point' and 'Waterloo Staithes' both adjoining the river . . .

Coal in abundance arrives also daily from the south, in the neighbourhood of Wakefield, brought in ordinary carts along the turnpike road. Besides the channels already cited, another has lately been opened by the Selby Railroad, in consequence of which undertaking, and the facility of delivery

In 1812 the great Leeds engineer Matthew Murray built the world's first commercially successful locomotive in order to haul coal into Leeds from the Middleton collieries at a time when the Napoleonic Wars had caused a great shortage of horses. Nathaniel Whittock's view of 1829 shows one of these locomotives on the coal staithes near Meadow Lane. Here the coal was shot out of the waggons, through holes in the arches, to fall down into horse-drawn delivery waggons waiting beneath.

resulting from it, new staithes have been constructed within the premises of that establishment, and new shafts have already been sunk on the line, which latter will, ere long, contribute largely to the general stock . . .

The supply of building stone it the vicinity of Leeds is no less abundant than that of coal. The banks of the Liverpool Canal especially are continually covered with the material in all various sizes and dimensions, such as large blocks, slabs for paving, as well as others of thinner dimensions, termed 'grey slate' for roofing dwellings, etc; the whole lying ready for embarkation and export to almost all parts of the country. The navigation to Liverpool by this canal is performed in about a week by the ordinary craft; the fly-boats occupy two days and three nights; the distance by water is one hundred and twenty miles; the number of locks is ninety-two. By the Aire and Calder navigation towards the east; the port of Goole is reached in nine hours, whence vessels proceed onwards by the Humber to the coast.

I rode to the quarries at Bramley Fall, three miles from Leeds on the south bank of the above canal; these occupy a slanting ridge of steep ground, covered with scrubby, stunted trees, the excavations being numerous, rather than large or deep.

A specimen of the stone, which is of excellent quality, and is quarried with remarkable facility, crumbling, as it were, spontaneously into large blocks, capable of being removed in their original shape without the trouble of blasting, may be seen in the balustrades of the new London Bridge.

The Woodhouse quarries, situated about a mile northward of the town, produce good sandstone. It is quarried easier, if possible, than that at Bramley Fall; not only lying naturally in horizontal layers, and splitting in a parallel direction by the slightest blow of the chisel, but from the alterations of temperature, or other causes it cracks perpetually in deep

fissures; in fact, the workmen have nothing to do but to raise the blocks from the quarries . . .

(He then visited the Coloured Cloth Hall)

. . .though the extend of the building is very remarkable, I know of no other elsewhere with which a place it in comparison. It rather resembles three sides of a square of house, than a single edifice. A long room, gallery or street, as it is most properly called, extends from one end to the other of each side; and in these covered ways, the cloth brought from the adjacent country by the domestic weavers, in an unfinished state, is exposed for sale to the manufacturers, who finish it by machinery. Two rows of tables, one on each side, are ranged the whole length of the building; on these the bales of cloth are laid, a wide space remaining in the middle, whereon the purchasers parade up and down. Matters are conducted with remarkable celerity, and as far as I could see, the first price offered generally adhered to. Few words go to a bargain; the cloth is first held up to the light, whipped with a small bundle of blanched sticks, and smoothed down once or twice by the hand, when the price is registered in a little narrow book, and the purchaser strides forward in quest of a fresh article.

Here men of business may receive a useful lesson in the art of making up their minds in a hurry; for the regulations of the establishment make dispatch indispensable and a short time only on two days in a week is dedicated to the cloth sales. On the mornings of Tuesday and Saturdays, the commencment of the market is proclaimed by the sound of a bell at half past eight o'clock in the morning. A few minutes before ten the same bell rings again, the latter being a signal to close the first part of the building, and commence on an upper floor. Twenty minutes is allowed here — the bell then rings a third time, and everybody is hustled out.

As soon as the Coloured Cloth Hall is closed, that for white undyed cloth, situated in another part of the town,

The Bazaar was built in the area of the present County Arcade in 1826. Its ground-level shops were all occupied by butchers, while the central doorway on this Briggate frontage led up to the bazaar itself, a room over 200ft long occupied by a variety of fancy goods and haberdashery stalls. It was demolished for redevelopment around 1900.

is then opened by a like signal . . .

In a walk through the streets of Leeds. I witnessed the performance of a piece of machinery employed in an unexpected, if not unusual service — that of chopping sausages; nevertheless the simplicity of the contrivance afforded fair grounds to consider why the same aid is not more generally applied to culinary purposes; moreover, I am by no means sure that such an instrument, on a small scale, might not be turned to the benefit of those who have lost their teeth — even entirely to supercede the knife and fork. One disadvantage is certainly to be complained of, namely, the grevious noise it makes while working; however, to this noise I am indebted for the opportunity of seeing it at all; for such was the rattling and thumping produced.

1835

Diary of Mrs Sarah Ellis, July 1835 *(Manuscript in private collection)*

Saturday morning, Mr E.I. and Mrs Slaughter, got in to a post chaise and EE road with the man that drove, set off a little before seven o'clock. Arrived at Hull just in time for the rail way packett, which we enter'd as soon as we left the chaise. We had a fine run to Selby, I am told about forty miles. At one place it was rather shallow, and two men on each side of the ship, having a long piece of wood mark'd a foot black and a foot white, plumb'd the depth of water for a considerable time. It was a little as seven foot at one time. Soon after we took a turn and got into a much narrower river and more depth of water. Feeling the air cool on Board,

I went down into the cabbin, which was paper'd with crimson damask paper, a table set out with plates of shrimps. At the bottom of the stairs was a little tap room, where we might be supplied with any thing we needed. We had a glass of wine good. I found a penny magazine and amused myself by reading the account of the diamond. Stopt several times to take in passengers; at length we landed at *Selby*. (As we past Brough we look'd and shook my handkerchief but no one could we see. We little thought then that Mrs Ellis was at Mr Beaumonts looking to make out the packett we was in but could not), and being directed, soon found the rail way coaches, got into one which holds six passengers, very roomy, with a piece of wood between each, flat at the top to lay your arm on. We went at rather a slow pace for that conveyance. I understand the ingine threw off the water very much; I think it might be so, as Elizabeth often said how the water sprincles in my face. They were oblig'd to stop to recruit with thick water, which caused it to make much noise. Took a young man with us which made five. We had to pass through a dark tunnel, of some length that was dismal. Got safe to Leeds, took an Omnibus which carried us to an Inn. Here we stopt till Monday. *Leeds* is a fine town, but very dirty and dusty, and so was the Inn. It was markett day, we could see the stalls out of our window, as we drove along in the Omnibus, I saw a great number of shoestalls; I concluded it was of no use to count them, for they increased as we went. I think there was not so much earthen ware as at Hull, one stall before the Inn had oranges and lemons to sell. I went out and bought two oranges for sixpence; they were fine large ones. In the evening went with Mrs S. and E. to see a Bazzaar; it was like going into a large 'hall fill'd with shops, some for toys, some with caps and collars etc., some with Jewelry, and various things besides. We walk'd round the bottom part, then ascended the stairs, which was in like manner occupied; one person had a very long shop. I thought she must look sharp when she was at one end, that she was not rob'd at the other. I purchased a pair of chamber Bellows here, as I wish'd for something to remember Leeds. It was getting so dusky I was troubled to see. Mrs S. made some little purchase, I think a pair of salts; we then return'd to the Inn, and found the markett which we had to pass thro' — very busy. Sunday, went to Salem chaple. where the late Mr Parsons preache'd, and heard Mr Eleg, from Rom. 8 and 18. He seem'd to choose it as consolation to a bereaved family of the church; he is a man of good ability, and has a good voice, very pritty, but I did not feel it. We went in the afternoon, he preach'd from Tim 3 and 16, it was their ordinance day I perceived, as there was something cover'd up on the table. We three women stopt and went up into the Gallery, now we saw the table spread and all the vessels exposed to view, 4 cups in 4 plates, two high Tankerds with covers in plates; 4 plates with bread out or broke ready, with two pieces of bread laid in those plates nearest to him, which I saw him brake at the beginning. I think it was all silver, the cups wash'd with gold. He prayed and spoke a little, while he was breking the bread amongst the rest he said; after prayer he handed the bread to the 4 Deacons and the Clark, who only sat in the table pew with him, and took of the same himself. When they had set a while the 4 Deacons rose and took each a plate and went round to the people; when they return'd they partook of the wine first, and then carried it round as before. I was much pleased with the proprosity of his conduct — he spoke not while the clements were distributing — I should think them was 150 or 200 membrs; solidity and reverence mark'd the place; we sang an hymn and came away. At night we went to hear a Mr Acworth, a Baptist Minister; he did not preach, but I suppose a scotch man as he said he came from Dundee. When he rose to pray, near all the people sat on their seats, which I think show'd a want of reverence, I have forgot where his text was, but it was a long one out of one of the gosples. His sermon had nothing to do with his text, and more, I thought he said somethings erronious. I could not help thinking he was an imposter. We came out before he had done, and glad to make our escape. I should have said on Saturday, we took a walk to find a house that Mr Slaughter sold some hops to last year, and he wish'd Mrs S. to call and enquire if they wanted any more. When we came to it, Mr E. and Mrs S. went in and was to walk gently back. I wish'd to call at a shop and sit till they came, but as were going along saw a markett place, so we went and set down there, after I had spread my handkerchief on the seat, least it should soil my gown. When we saw Mr E. and Mrs S. pass we hastend away and I forgot my handkerchief; thought no more of it till we had got near to the Inn, so I left that behind as I thought it would be gone before I got there. It was a small white handkerchief with red border. Monday, set off early in a stage from the Inn.

1837

Barclay Fox (1817-1855) was the brother of the Quaker diarist Caroline Fox and a member of a prominent Falmouth family, which had business interests in shipping, mining and fishing. He kept his Journal from 1832 until his marriage in 1844, and describes

in it 'life in Cornwall and his travels in Britain' and Italy'.
Brett, R.L. (ed) *Barclay Fox's Journal* (London 1979).

(Leeds) amongst all others of its species is the vilest of the vile. At a mile distant from the town we came under a vast dingy canopy formed by the impure exhalation of a hundred furnaces. It sits on the town like an everlasting incubus, shutting out the light of heaven and the breath of summer. I pity its poor denizens. London is a joke to it. Our inn was consistant with its locality; one doesn't look for a clean floor in a colliery or a decent hotel in Leeds. (12th) Made various fruitless enquiries for Jos. Peace & others of Mother's friends, but no satisfactory information could we obtain. The inhabitants are as dull as lead and the smoke 'has entered into their souls'. After breakfast we visited the huge woollen mart, containing upwards of a thousand sellers' stalls. Piles of broad cloth everywhere met our view, guarded by a regiment of wool dealers armed with little brooms to defend their goods from flies and furnace dust. The whole spot was pervaded with a close clothy smell, but the heavy countenances of the dealers seemed well adapted to their scene of action. We left this dingy town directly afterwards and in about 3 miles travelling got beyond the influence of its murky atmosphere.
24 August, 1844
Reached Leeds at 8. I put up at Scarborough's and ordered a fire in lieu of female society. What a 10 days I have had!

25th
William burst into my room between 6 and 7 looking like a windmill. Heartily glad were we to meet, and gladder still to be sitting over a comfortable breakfast in his parlour about an hour later.

1842

Robert Baker (1803-1880), CB, MRCS, became town surgeon of Leeds in 1825. His pioneering reports of 1832 and 1839 on the Leeds cholera epidemics showed the connection between the virulence of the disease and the insanitary condition of the town. One of the first to be appointed a factory doctor to examine the workers, he became Sub-Inspector of Factories in 1834 and one of only two Inspectors of Factories in 1858. His 1842 Report, of which this is a small sample, was included in the Poor Law Commissioners' report on the sanitary condition of the labouring population of England.
Baker, R.
On the state and condition of the town of Leeds in the West-Riding of the County of York (Leeds, 1842) p.1-6.

The town of Leeds, in the West Riding of the County of York is situated on the River Aire, which runs through it, and which is navigable only hitherto. It forms by far the most important of the 11 townships of which the borough is composed, having, by the census of 1841, a population of 87,613 persons out of a parochial and total population of 150,587. The acres of the parish or borough are stated to be 21,450, but the total acreage of the township is only 2,672 A.2R.

By the Municipal Act of Will, IV., the borough of Leeds was divided into 12 wards of which eight are in the township of Leeds viz., the North, North-east, East, South, Kirkgate, Millhill, West and North-west.

The town itself stands on sloping ground, the highest part of which is on Woodhouse Moor, to the West, and which is about 232 feet above the level of the River Aire below the Hunslet Weir.

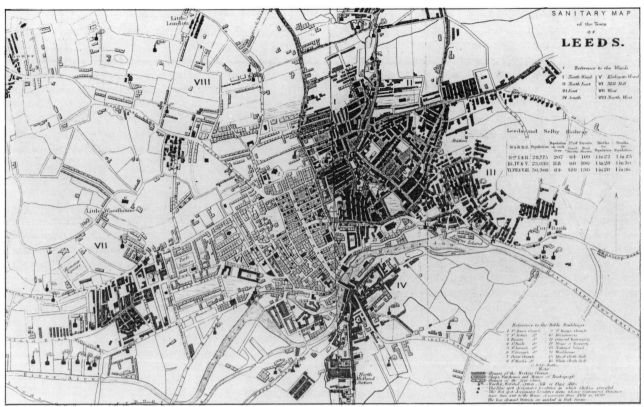

This map was prepared as part of Robert Baker's 1842 report on the unsanitary state of Leeds. it clearly shows the light-coloured area of healthy first-rate housing in the Georgian west end, sandwiched between the dark-coloured industrial suburbs where poor housing, cholera and other contagious diseases flourished. Note too the concentrations of factories on Kirkstall Road, Holbeck and the Bank.

By the 1830s the industrial areas of Leeds all suffered from polluted air, polluted water, and vast accummulations of grime and insanitary waste. The once crystal-clear river Aire was now being fouled by industrial and human effluent, 'so exhalent and noisome as to be offensive in the first degree'. Here Charles Cope shows the town from the east, with Leeds Lock and Leeds Dam in the middle distance, then the chimney of the oil mills, with the tower of the parish church rising above Nether Mills. At the extreme right are Bank Mills.

The Hunslet Weir is here mentioned, because it is only below this, a distance down the river of about two miles, that an effectual drainage can be obtained.

Within it are going on daily the processes of flax-spinning and weaving by hand; the manufacture of woollen cloths, and of some worsted goods; of various kinds of machinery, of tobacco, and pipes, dye-works; ware and saw-mills, and other processes of industry.

The higher parts of the town are ordinarily clean for so large a manufacturing location; but the lower parts, which lie contiguous to the river and the Becks or rivulets are dirty, confined, ill ventilated, and in many instances self-sufficient to shorten life, and especially infant life, when exposed to their influence.

The comparatively little sewerage of the town is emptied into the river and the Timble Bridge beck, a rivulet which runs from north-west to south-east, joining the river in the East ward. The river and this beck are so much the receptacles of all kinds of refuse, that long before either of them reach the town, their waters are perfectly discoloured. With the river it is not so much the case but with the Timble Bridge beck running through the most important ward of the Town in point of population, the refuse left upon its sides, on its waters being drawn off for particular purposes, is so exhalant and noisome as to be offensive in the first degree. Some idea may be formed of the use of its waters by engines and dye-houses, that serious contentions have occasionally arisen between parties appropriating them for condensing purposes, on account of their heat.

The lower parts of the town are furthermore disgusting, particularly on account of a general want of paving and draining, for the irregularity of their buildings, for the violation of the common decencies of life in the abundance of refuse and excrementitious matter lying about in various directions, and what is indeed a matter of universal complain in every part of Leeds, for the pavement, where there is any, being set in ashes, and occasionally covered with the same, by which, in dry weather, a black and irritating dust prevails, not only in the streets but the houses; and in dirty weather, a spunging puddle, most foul and most offensive.

It might be imagined that at least the streets over which the town surveyors have a legal right to exercise control, would be sewered, but this is not the case; of the 68 streets, which they superintend, 19 are not sewered at all, and 10 are only partly so; nay, it is only within the three or four years past that a sewer has been completed through the main street for two of the most populous wards of the town, embracing together a population of 30,540 persons, by which a carry off the surface and drainage-water of an elevation of 150 feet, where, indeed, there could be no excuse for want of sufficient fall. I have seen, in the neighbourhood to which I now refer, an attempt made to drain the cottage houses into a small drain passing under the causeway, and which afterwards had to be continued, through a small sewer, and through private property, by a circuitous route, in order to reach its natural outlet, and the water from the surveyor's drain regurgitate into the cutting from the dwellings. It only needs to be pointed out that the sewer which has subseuqently been made, and is most effective, is an evidence of the previous practicability of a work so essential to the welfare of the people; but I may add, that many of the inhabitants of the districts a little further distant from the town, where fever is always rife, are yet obliged to use cesspools, which are constructed under their very doors, for the want of the continuation of this desirable measure.

Along the line of these two wards, and down the street which divides them, and where this sewer has been recently made, numbers of streets have been formed and houses erected, without pavement, and hence without surface-drainage, without sewers, or if under-drainage can be called sewers, then with such as, becoming choked in a few months, are even worse than if they were altogether without. The surface of these streets is considerably elevated by accumulated ashes and filth, untouched by any scavenger; they form nuclei of disease exhaled from a thousand sources. Here and there

stagnant water, and channels so offensive that they have been declared to be unbearable, lie under the doorways of the uncomplaining poor; and privies so laden with ashes and excrementitious matter, as to be unuseable, prevail, till the streets themselves become offensive from deposits of this description: in short there is generally pervading these localities a want of the common conveniences of life.

The courts and *culs-de-sac* exist everywhere. The building of house back to back occasions this in a great measure. It is in fact part of the economy of buildings that are to pay a good per centage. In one *cul-de-sac*, in the town of Leeds, there are 34 houses, and in ordinary times, there dwell in these houses 340 persons, or ten to every house; but as these houses are many of them receiving-houses for itinerant labourers during the periods of hay-time and harvest, and the fairs, at least twice that number are then here congregated. The name of this place is the Boot and Shoe-yard, in Kirkgate, a location, from whence the Commissioners removed, in the days of the cholera, 75 cartloads of manure, which had been untouched for years, and where there now exists a surface of human excrement, of very considerable extent, to which these impure and unventilated dwellings are additionally exposed. This property is said to pay the best annual interest of any cottage property in the borough.

1842

J.G.Kohl was a German traveller who toured England in the autumn and winter of 1842, his methodical and detailed travelogue providing a fascinating description of England by an intelligent outside observer.
Kohl, J.G. *England, Wales and Scotland* (1844) p.100-104.

Leeds, like its brethren, Sheffield, Manchester, and the other great manufacturing cities of England, can boast of no interesting antiquities, no historical associations, no classical appelation like that of 'Eboracum', the Roman name for York. But it has many peculiar and interesting features to boast of, perhaps quite as valuable as any of these.

Leeds is the central point of the English woollen manufacture. There are, indeed, woollen manufactories in Gloucester, Somerset, and Wiltshire, but they are unimportant in comparison with those of Bradford, Wakefield, Huddersfield, Halifax, and above all, Leeds. Three-fourths of the woollen-cloth produced in England is manufactured in the West Riding of Yorkshire.

I visited the Cloth-Hall of Leeds, which consists of a plain quadrangular house, containing long spacious galleries, in which the cloth-makers display their wares for sale. The house is damp and foggy, but this pleases the cloth-makers, because it is softening and beneficial to their wares. The galleries are divided, on both sides into little cells, called 'stands', about twenty-two inches wide, in which the sellers are stationed, with a path down the middle, through which the buyer walks. Each stand is the property of a manufactorer, who has bought it and who may sell it when he pleases.

The regulations of the Cloth-hall are rather curious; there are only two market-days, Saturday and Tuesday, and even on these days, the time for transacting business is rigorously limited to precisely eighty minutes. The meaning of this is to same time, by promoting the rapid and energetic despatch of business. It is found that in this short time, as much, nay, perhaps more business is done, than in the former longer periods; for no time is now wasted in hesitation or daly, but both buyer and seller say at once what they mean, and lose neither words nor minutes over their bargains. I would fain put this whole paragraph in italics, fo the benefit of my German countrymen, who might borrow a useful hint from he busy Cloth-hall of Leeds. The enormous mass of business transacted there during the year, requires, in consequence of these regulations, only about 135 hours.

The sellers in these cloth-halls are principally the smaller manufacturers, living in the neighbouring villages, who here sell their wares to the great 'cloth-dressers', by whom it is finished-off, packed, and exported. There is some cloth which never comes into the cloth-halls at all, but is privately sold by the weavers to the great dealers.

It is rather strange, that with all which the improvement of machinery has done to promote the 'factory-system', there should still exist, as is the case, so many little weaving-establishments, entirely independant of the great manufacturers.

During the last forty years, the number of the former has even increased, although not in the same proportion with that of the great factories. Perhaps the fact is, that many branches of the business can never be so well carried on in the factories as in the houses of the weavers. In bad times their number generally increases, probably because the great manufacturers are soonest and most powerfully affected by disastrous conjunctures, and their labourers thrown out of employment, often set up for themselves in a small way of business.

During the late bad years, from 1838 to 1841, it is computed that the amount of wages paid was on an average, 27,071, sterling less every week, than during the period from 1833 to 1835. The number of oxen, pigs, and sheep, consumed every week in Leeds during 1835, was 2450; in the year 1841, it was only 1800! Yet a Leeds manufacturer told me that wages had fallen much less at Leeds than at Manchester, and that the inhabitants of Leeds had also remained much more quiet. The swarms of insurgent workmen came all from Manchester.

At Leeds I went over some of the great factories, in which the wool is carried through its various processes. One of these manufactories is considered to be among the most perfect of its kind in England. The whole arrangements of the establishment, the elegance, solidity, and size of the machines, surpassed any thing I had seen before. I was shown two spinning-jennies, of which each spun 520 bobbins. Two workmen were thus enabled to superintend 1040 bobbins. I could scarcely believe this; but giving myself the trouble to count them, I found the number exact. The son of the manufacturer, who accompanied me, assured me that in one week a thread 40,000 miles long could be spun in their manufactory. At this rate they could 'put a girdle round about the earth', if not in 'forty minutes', yet in little more than three days.

Leeds, like all the great manufacturing cities of England, is a dirty, smoky, disagreeable town. Though its streets are laid out on a regular plan, there are very few neat rows of houses to be seen, because the factories take up a great deal of room, and do not submit to any regular arrangement. The streets are not all paved, and no provision has yet been made for the regular carrying off of mud and rain-water. The River Aire, which runs through the town in different canals, is everywhere thick and dirty, in consequence of the various contributions made to its waters, from all the different manufactories. The attention of parliament has lately been drawn to this state of the city, and many provisions for its improvements have been made. Among other regulations it has been enacted that all the factories should provide themselves, before the 1st of January 1843, with chimneys for perfect combustion, by which Leeds will be spared the infliction of much of their noxious smoke.

Though the woollen fabric is the principal employment

of Leeds and its vicinity, many other sorts of factories are there to be found. Leeds contains chemical works of various kinds, leather, mustard, and brush manufactories, and glass works, and potteries of different kinds, many of which I visited, and in all of which I saw or heard something that was both new and interesting to me.

The manufacturing cities of England are none of them very attractive or pleasing in appearance, but Leeds is, perhaps, the ugliest and least attractive town in all England. In Birmingham, Manchester, and other such cities, among the mass of chimney sand factories, are scattered, here and there, splendid newsrooms, or clubs, and interesting exchanges, banks, railway-stations or Wellington and Nelson monuments. Leeds has none of these. I was, therefore not sorry when after seeing what interested me in the manufactories of Leeds, the time came for me to seat myself once more in one of those cheerful and comfortable flying-houses (railway carriages) in which I scarcely ever failed to enjoy, besides their own comforts, the society of some communicative and interesting fellow-traveller; for stiff and reserved as the English are said to be to each other, I have always found them, in their own country, friendly, hospitable, and sociable towards the traveller and the stranger.

1843

T.J.Maslen was a retired officer of the East India Company (he was a Lieutenant in the Native Infantry, Fort St George, in 1816) who published a 'Plan for exploring the interior, and for carrying out a survey of the whole continent of Australia' in 1830. His graphic description of Leeds in 1843 is followed by a suggestion for the creation of a unified Headrow which might have been taken as the blueprint for the building of the street in the 1920s and 1930s.
Maslen T.J. *Suggestions for the improvement of our towns and houses* (1843) pp.98-115

I shall also just notice the pretty condition of the river Aire, which runs through Leeds. Instead of being an ornament to the town, and a minister of pleasures to its citizens, by boating, swimming and fishing, its banks are crowded and shut up with buildings, and its waters are like a reservoir of poison, carefully kept for the purpose of breeding a pestilence in the town. In that part of the river, extending from Armley mills to the King's mills, it is charged with the drainage and contents of about two hundred water-closets, cesspools, and privies, a great number of common drains, the drainings from dung-hills, the infirmary, (dead leeches, poultices for patients, &c.,) slaughter-houses, chemical soap, gas, drug, dye-houses, and manufacturers, spent blue and black dye, pig-manure, old urine wash, with all sorts of dead animal and vegetable substances, and now and then a decomposed human body; forming an annual mass of filth equal to thirty millions of gallons! This was, until lately, the delicious nectar, the delectable water that went to make tea, to be carried to the lips of the beautiful young ladies of Leeds, (and they are the loveliest girls in the world) and to cook the victuals of the inhabitants. But, although the town is now furnished with purer water for every purpose, yet the condition of the river remains the same, evolving a diurnal exhalation of disease as regularly as the sun rises in the heavens, and I am afraid it will continue to do so until the better judgement of the wealthy mill-owners prompts them to remove their factories and other buildings further down the river, away from the town. It would be better for the work-people to have to go half a mile out of the town to their work in the mills and factories, than to have the health and cleanliness of the town spoilt by the factories being suffered to be erected in the town. And it is also better for people to congregate and live together in cities and towns, (away from the manufactories), as the association of large numbers of people together, tends to civilization and enlightenment, breeds friendships and mutual acts of benevolence . . .

When I visited Leeds, I must confess I was astonished at the filthiness of the town, and the glaring apathy and neglect that was observable in the building-schemes that were carrying on, (especially in the North and West quarters, where upwards of two dozen little new streets, or attempts at new streets, are run up in all manner of directions, without any regular plan or imaginable motive but to create confusion or a labyrinth, amidst holes and hillocks, ponds and puddles, and mud a yard deep.

Many respectable houses in this town have no gardens, nor even back courts, nor scarcely a foot of ground attached to them except a little tiny front court enclosed with an iron-railing; and yet great rents were demanded for these suicidal prisons (and they deserve no better name), for whoever takes such houses, must submit to linger out life without one of its principal enjoyments, a spot of shrubbery and fresh air; and to be retired, it should be at the back of the house. The houses in Rockingham-street, Coburg-street, Queen-square, and every other street and square in the town might have had, and ought to have had, back gardens, a morsel larger than their present ones, if they had been built by considerate, liberal-minded and humane men, who remembered they were building habitations for human beings and not cages for beasts. I went to Leeds with the full determination of taking a house and establishing myself there, but I quitted the town in disgust . . .

At some future time a great thoroughfare will be found to be necessary from East to West in the northern parts of Leeds, and it would be wise to begin early and provide a grand wide street for that purpose. The best line that at present offers for its formation is Park-Lane, Guilford-Street, Upper Head-row, Lower Head-row and Lady-Lane; and thus form a junction with Quarry-hill. This grand thoroughfare should be thirty yards wide throughout.

1843

John Marshall (1765-1845) had worked with a great Leeds engineer Matthew Murray to develop efficient flax-spinning machinery in the 1790s. As Leeds developed as the centre of the world's flax-spinning industry, Marshall's Mills of 1792 had already been extended five times before their vast new addition in the Egyptian style was built in 1838-40.
'A Day at a Leeds Flax-Mill (Marshall's) '*Penny Magazine* XII (1843) pp.501-8.

Messrs Marshall, of Leeds, to whose courtesy and kindness we are indebted on the present occasion, have a flax-mill in that town which is among the largest factories in the empire. It gives employment to no less than twenty-three hundred persons, and in it also is prepared the yarn from which thread is made by seven hundred persons employed in another factory owned by the same firm at Shrewsbury; thus making three thousand operatives engaged in the various stages in the preparation of flax . . .

The flax-mill which we are about to visit is situated in a south-western suburb of Leeds, called Holbeck, on the south of the river Aire. The buildings comprising it are scattered over an area of many acres, and exhibit to view an asemblage

The new flax mill built in 1838-40 by Messrs Marshall in Marshall Street, Holbeck, was one of the most outstanding architectural products of the industrial revolution. Behind its vast Egyptian façade, modelled on the temple of Horus at Edfu, lay a two-acre factory (to the left) and an office block (to the right). Even the great chimney in the background took the form and proportion of the huge Egyptian obelisk known as Cleopatra's Needle. This mid nineteenth-century drawing is the work of W.R.Robinson.

of structures of different sizes and ages, resembling a little town which has grown with the growth of its manufactures, not on any very symmetrical plan, but as convenience from time to time suggested . . .

On proceeding down Marshall Street, we first pass a long range of dark brick buildings, forming the main portion of the old mill; and then we come to an open space between the old and new mills, with an arched passage leading from the one to the other. In this opening, or rather somewhat behind it, is situated the tall chimney of the new mill, a chimney having the form and proportions of the oft-described 'Cleopatra's Needle' of Egypt. We next come to a building, not yet entirely finished, which is to form the offices and counting-houses of the factory; exhibiting a front analogous to that of an Egyptian temple, derived from the drawings and designs of Bonomi and David Roberts. Then we arrive at the mill itself, which exhibits on the eastern side a facade one storey in height, a range of eighteen windows, very much larger than are customarily used in factories, a range of eighteen pillars of pilasters, and a kind of projecting cornice running along the top; the whole having an Egyptian character in the general appearance and arrangement, and the whole front being formed of stone. The other sides exhibit externally nothing remarkable, if we except the great length.

Let us next visit the interior. Here the eye takes in at a glance an amount of space which, we believe, no room devoted to manufactures anywhere else exhibits. Indeed this is one of the largest rooms in the world. It measures three hundred and ninety-six feet long by two hundred and sixteen broad, covering nearly two acres of ground . . .

The room presents to view about fifty pillars placed equidistant and supporting the roof. This roof is formed of brick, and consists of sixty-six feet flattish domes or groined arches, each about thrity-six feet span. In the centre of each arch is a skylight of large dimensions, being thirteen or fourteen feet in diameter, and rising conically to a height of eight or nine feet above the roof, thus presenting on the whole a surface of ten thousand square feet of glazed skylight, by which a very efficient light is admitted to the room. As the room is about twenty feet high, there is a degree of airiness, or freedom in the atmosphere (if we may use such a term), not often observable in factories. Although the machines in the room are very numerous, yet so ample in the space left between the avenues along which they are ranged, that the eye glances along the vista uninterruptedly, there being several parallel ranges of machines extending the entire length of nearly four hundred feet . . .

When we descent beneath this great room, we find a series of vaults and passages, all formed of substantial brickwork, employed chiefly in regulating the warmth and ventilation of the rooms above. There is a steam-engine of eight horse-power which forces air through ranges of pipe in two large steam-chests, where it become Sheated, and is from thence conveyed up into the mill. There is also an arrangement of valves and doors by which the air is brought to any desired temperature according to the season; or it may have imparted to it any degree of mositure best suited to the preparation of the flax. The ventilation is aided by valvular openings at the summits of the conical skylights. The vaults also contain the shafts for communicating to the room above the motion from a pair of very large steam-engines.

Having gone beneath the giant-room, we may next go

This view of the interior of Marshall's Mill is taken from The Penny Magazine *of 1832. It clearly shows the domed roof with its numerous skylights, and the spinning machinery driven by shafts running beneath the floor.*

above it; and here a stranger is apt to be puzzled in no small degree. To 'take a walk in the fields' on the top of a factory seems strange enough, yet such is the impression likely to be made at a first glance. The whole surface is covered with full and luxuriant grass, not artificially smooth like a lawn, but with such slight undulations of level as make the resemblance to a field more striking. If a visitor were to go on the roof before seeing the inside of the building, he would infallibly think that the room had been excavated out of the solid ground; and the sixty or seventy skylights, rising up conically from the grass induce him to ponder whether any gardening operations are being carried on; whether these glass enclosures — a sort of hybrid between cucumber-frames and greenhouse — are the scene of any experimental researches on plants. On looking down one of these skylights, however, the spindles and bobbins are seen working away by thousands; and the inquiry then naturally suggests itself why this form of roof has been adopted. The brick arches which form the ceiling of the great room are covered with a layer of rough plaster, then with an impermeable coating of lime and coal-tar, as a kind of asphalte; and in order to prevent the heat of the sun from crackling this composition, a layer of about eight inches of good mould is laid over, and grass-seed sown therein . . .

When on the roof of the mill, we can see a neat red brick building which forms the School belonging to the factory . . .

The schoolhouse has been built expressly for its present object. It contains, besides private apartments for the master and mistress, a boys' school-room measuring eighty feet by thirty-six, a girls' school-room nearly as large, and a class-room for lectures, &c. between the two. One of the rooms contains an organ. In the boys' school there are benches arranged on the class or monitorial system, each bench having a kind of shelf beneath it, on which the boys place their caps, and a monitor's seat which is also a box for containing books. Although intended principally for the factory children, yet these schools are open to all the children in the neighbourhood of the factory, whose parents choose to adopt the regulations laid down for its good governance . . .

Altogether there are about three hundred and fifty boys, and a hundred and eight girls, who are under the care of a master and mistress engaged expressly for the school. The school rooms are comfortably warmed by hot-water apparatus; and there is a large plot of ground outside the building which serves as a play-ground. As to the internal discipline of the schools, there is the same busy hum, the same thumbing of slates, pencils, and books, the same mixture of the slow-moving with the quick-moving intellect, of the meek and placid boy while the young rogue who looks as if he loved marbles better than books, as in most schools. The boys mostly wear a kind of short pinafore made of coarse flaxen cloth, called a 'harding' or 'harden'; and their appearance on the whole is certainly indicative of good health and high animal spirits.

1844

Friedrick Engels (1820-1895) was the son of a German cotton manufacturer who came to Manchester in 1842 as agent for his father's company. Here he gathered information for his *Condition of the Working Classes in England*, and developed a life-long friendship with Marx, with whom he produced the famous *Communist Manifesto* in London 1845.
Engels, F. *The Condition of the Working Class in England in 1844.* (1892 ed) pp.39, 40, 157.

The valleys of the Aire, along which stretches Leeds, and of the Calder, through which the Manchester-Leeds railway runs, are among the most attractive in England, and are strewn in all directions with the factories, villages, and towns. The houses of rough grey stone look so neat and clean in comparison with the blackened brick buildings of Lancashire, that it is a pleasure to look at them. But on coming into the towns themselves, one finds little to rejoice over. Leeds lies as the *Artisan* describes it, and as I found confirmed upon examination: 'on a gentle slope that descends into the valley of the Aire. This stream flows through the city for about a mile-and-a-half and is exposed to violent floods during thaws or heavy rain. The higher western portions of the city are clean, for such a large town. But the low-lying districts along the river and its tributary becks are narrow, dirty, and enough to themselves to shorten the lives of the inhabitants, especially of little children. Added to this, the disgusting state of the working-men's districts about Kirkgate, Marsh Lane, Cross Street and Richmond Road, which is chiefly attributable to their unpaved, drainless streets, irregular architecture, numerous courts and alleys, and total lack of the most ordinary means of cleanliness, all this taken together is explanation enough of the excessive mortality in these unhappy abodes of filthy misery. In consequence of the overflows of the Aire, (which, it must be added, like all other rivers in the service of manufacture, flows into the city at one end clear and transparent, and flows out at the other end thick black and foul, smelling of all possible refuse), 'the houses and cellars are often so full of water that they have to be pumped out. And at such times the water rises, even where there are sewers, out of them into cellars, engenders miasmatic vapours strongly impregnated with sulphurette hydrogen, and leaves a disgusting residuum highly injurious to health. During the spring-floods in 1839, the action of such a choking of the sewers was so injurious, that, according to the report of the Registrar of Births and Deaths for this part of the town, there were three deaths to two births, whereas in the same three months, in every other part of the town, there were three births to two deaths. Other thickly populated districts are without any sewers whatsoever, or so badly provided as to derive no benefit from them. In some rows of houses the cellars are seldom dry; in certain districts there are several streets covered with soft mud a foot deep. The inhabitants have made vain attempts from time to time to repair these streets with shovelfuls of cinders, but in spite of all such attempts, dung-heaps, and pools of dirty water emptied from the houses, fill all the holes until wind and sun dry them up. An ordinary cottage in Leeds occupies not more than five yards square of land, and usually contracted dwellings, filled day and night with human beings, are another point dangerous alike to the morals and the health of the inhabitants'. And how greatly these cottages are crowded the Report on the Health of the Working-Classes, quoted above, bears testimony: 'In Leeds we found brothers and sisters and lodgers of both sexes, sharing the parents' sleeping-room, whence arise consequences at the contemplation of which human feeling shudders' . . .

F.Sharp in Leeds, the surgeon already quoted:
"When I moved from Scarborough to Leeds, I was at once struck by the fact that the general appearance of the children was much paler, and their fibre less vigorous here than in Scarborough and its environs. I saw, too, that many children were exceptionally small for their age. I have met with numberless cases of scrofula, lung trouble, mesenteric affections, and indigestion, concerning which I, as a medical man, have no doubt that they arose from mill work. I believe

'Leeds, like all the great manufacturing cities of England, is a dirty, smoky, disagreeable town' wrote J.G.Kohl in 1844. This drawing of Leeds from the Whitehall Road, made by Henry Burn just two years later, shows how the open fields of Holbeck had been swamped by industrial development over the last half century. Marshalls Mills dominate the centre of the scene, with the towers of the Parish Church to the left, and Christ Church, Meadow Lane, to the right.

that the nervous energy of the body is weakened by the long hours, and the foundation of many diseases laid. If people from the country were not constantly coming in, the race of mill-hands would soon be wholly degerate.'

1845

Smith, J. 'REPORT on the CONDITION of the TOWN of LEEDS' *Appendix to Second Report of Commissioners of Inquiry into the State of Large Towns and Populous Districts* (1844-45) p.312-20.
Houses, 33,902: population, 168,000; deaths, 2.7` per cent; excess in number of deaths in 1841, 1169; average age of all who died, 23 years 4 months; of adults, 51 years 1 month; proportion of infant deaths under 5 years to total deaths, 30.5 per cent.

Leeds: The town of Leeds is situated on the right and left banks of the River Aire, a navigable river in the West Riding of Yorkshire. The town lies chiefly on a slope of considerable acclivity, running towrds the south-east from the margin of the river. The sub-strata of the site of this part of the town are of the coal measures, and the surface covering is a tenacious clay of several feet in depth; the rock coming near the surface in some places. The general character of the subsoil is retentive. On the opposite side of the river, stretching towards the west there is an extensive flat, on which a considerable extent of buildings has in late times been erected, and the chief extension of the town is now taking place in that direction. This is called the Holbeck and Hunslet districts. This flat is traversed by two brooks (the Holbeck and Hunslet), which form the natural main sewers of the district. The flow of water is, however, retarded by various artificial obstructions which cause frequent overflowing of the ground, and at all times, retain masses of putrescent matter in the channels of the brooks. The natural flow of the River

Aire is obstructed by weirs placed across for navigation and mill purposes; the consequence of which is, that the water of the river is kept very much in still pools, and the lower streets and houses on the margin are flooded occasionally. Some water-courses for mill purposes, called "The Calls", pass along a considerable distance near the margin of the river, causing floodings and damp.

The obstructions in the river have also the effect of overflowing the outlets of the Holbeck and Hunslet brooks on the north-west side of the river, and consequently the whole natural drainage, and the sewerage flowing into these brooks is obstructed. In some places the banks of those brooks have been raised above the level of the adjoining general surface, causing damp and preventing a proper sewerage. In a district so flat and extensive as this, there are no means of obtaining a perfect drainage and sewerage, without a main level brought from a lower point of the river.

The general arrangement of the streets and alleys of Leeds are in the older parts very much as in all old towns, somewhat irregular and narrow; but, fortunately for Leeds, the main street is of ample width, arising, as I was told from a practice of the olden time, of having gardens in front of the houses, the area of which has in later times been added to the street. The row of streets running parallel to the river are, however, narrow, crooked, and irregular. Streets more recently formed are more ample in width, and there are many very cheerful open streets where the better classes reside. The lower classes here, as elsewhere, inhabit the less comfortable and less healthy localities along both sides of the Addle Beck, a stream which intersects the eastern division of the town, and which is obstructed by many weirs and bridges of limited openings, and by the encroachment of buildings on its bed. A great number of dye-houses and other manufactories are erected on the margin, and interspersed with them. A number of dwellings, which, from the damp and the pestilent effluvia from the decaying matter in the bottom of the Beck, combined with the smoke and fumes arising from the various works, are most unhealthy. But by far the most unhealthy localities of Leeds are close squares of houses, or yards, as they are called, which have been erected for the accommodation of working people. Some of these, though situated in comparatively high ground, are airless from the enclosed structure, and being wholly unprovided with any form of under-drainage, or convenience, or arrangements for cleansing, are one mass of damp and filth. In some instances I found cellars, or under-rooms, with from two to six inches of water standing over the floors, and putrid from its stagnation in one case, from receiving the soakage of the slop water standing in pools in the street adjoining. The ashes, garbage, and filth of all kinds are thrown from the doors and windows of the houses upon the surface of the streets and courts; and in some cases, where a gallery of entrance has been erected, for the inhabitants of the second floor, the whole of the slops and filth are thrown over the gallery in front of the houses beneath, and as the ground is often sloping towards the doors of the lower dwellings, they are inundated with water and filth, and the poor inhabitants placed in a miserable and unhealthy condition. The privies, as usual in such situations, are few in proportion to the number of inhabitants. They are open to view both in front and rear, are invariably in a filthy condition, and often remain without the removal of any portion of the filth for six months. The feelings of the people are blunted to all seeming decency, and from the constantly contaminated state of the atmosphere, a vast amount of ill health prevails, leading to listlessness, and inducing a desire for spirits and opiates; the combined influence of the whole condition causing much loss of time, increasing poverty, and terminating the existence of many in premature death. Mr Baker, a medical practitioner of Leeds, and for many years one of the council, published a few years ago a treatise on the vital statistics of Leeds, going very fully into this subject, and he has demonstrated very clearly and undeniably, from facts observed during a long residence, the evil effects of bad ventilation, bad drainage, and deficient supplies of water.

Many of the streets, alleys, and courts are unpaved, and some paved in a very imperfect manner. They are full of ruts and hollows holding water and filth. All vacant spaces of building ground are left undrained, and unenclosed, and with uneven surfaces, and in many cases the slop water from the neighbouring dwellings drains into them, creating extensive ponds of filthy water. All sorts of rubbish and filth are thrown upon these vacant spaces, and they become a wide field of effluvia and deleterious emanations. Pigsties are frequently erected upon them, and they are used as depots for dung by the much-gatherers. No cognizance is taken of their condition by the police.

In the Holbeck and Hunslet districts the streets have been laid off without reference to the best lines for drainage, and no systematic plan of drainage has been arranged. The river and the brooks over-flowing many portions of this district in rainy periods, and even in dry seasons the drainage is so imperfect as to leave stagnant pools of water in many of the streets and courts; and the houses having in general been set down without reference to any fixed levels, the lower floors of many are so far under the surface of the ground as to be continually damp. The greater number of the streets are unpaved, and consequently of uneven surface, full of ruts and hollows holding water; and as from the want of proper sewerage there are no house-drains, the slops and refuse from the houses are thrown upon the surface of the streets, which are in many places thereby raised some feet above the original level. All over this district the dunghills, ash-pits, and privies have been set down without any order,

in some places encroaching upon the streets, and in the courts the filth often covering almost the whole area.

1847

Charlotte Brontë (1816-1855), the famous author of *The Professor, Jane Eyre, Shirley* and *Villette* had personal experience of Leeds, which was one of the nearest major towns to her home on the edge of Haworth moor.
Brontë, C. *Jane Eyre* (1847) *('Millcote' is Leeds, the George Inn stood in Briggate, just to the south of the railway bridge).*

I longed to go where there was life and movement: Millcote was a large manufacturing town on the banks of the A---; a busy place enough, doubtless; so much the better, it would be a complete change at least. Not that my fancy was much captivated by the idea of long chimneys and clouds of smoke — 'but' — I argued, 'Thornfield will, probably, be a good way from the town' . . .

A new chapter in a novel is something like a new scene in a play; and when I draw up the curtain this time, reader, you must fancy you see a room in the George Inn at Millcote, with such large-figured papering on the walls as inn rooms have: such a carpet, such furniture, such ornaments on the mantel-piece, such prints; including a portrait of George the Third, and another of the Prince of Wales, and a representative of the death of Wolfe. All this is visible to you by the light of an oil-lamp hanging from the ceiling, and by that of an excellent fire, near which I sit in my cloak and bonnet; my muff and umbrella lie on the table, and I am warming away the numbness and chill contracted by sixteen hours' exposure to the rawness of an October day: I left Lowton at four o'clock P.M., and the Millcote town clock is now just striking eight . . .

(Later, from inside the departing coach) I let down the window and looked out: Millcote was behind us; judging by the number of its lights, it seemed a place of considerable magnitude, much larger than Lowton. We were now, as far as I could see, on a sort of common; but there were houses scattered all over the district: I felt we were in a different region to Lowood, more populous, less picturesque; more stirring, less romantic.

1848

Ralph Waldo Emerson (1803-1882), the American essayist and poet, first visited Europe in 1832, but this account of his experiences in Leeds was made during a subsequent visit in 1848. His hosts were the Revd. Wicksteed of Mill Hill Unitarian Chapel, who lived on Kingston Terrace, Francis Carbutt, wool importer of 10 Blenheim Square, the banker George Hyde at 69 Woodhouse Lane, and Joseph Lupton of 1 Blenheim Square.
Emerson, E.W. & Forbes, W.E. *Journals of Ralph Waldo Emerson 1845-1848 VIII* (1913) 379.

January 1848, Leeds.

Near Leeds and Bradford, I observed the sheep were black '& I fancied they were black sheep; no, they were begrimed by the smoke. So all the trees are begrimed. The human expectoration is black here, begrimed by the smoke . . .The hopelessness of keeping clothes white leads to a rather dowdy style of dress, I was told, among the ladies; and yet they sometimes indemnify themselves; and Leeds in the ballroom, I was assured, is a very different creature from Leeds in Briggate.

Mr Marshall's mill covers two acres of ground. The former owner, James Marshall, presided in this immense hall at

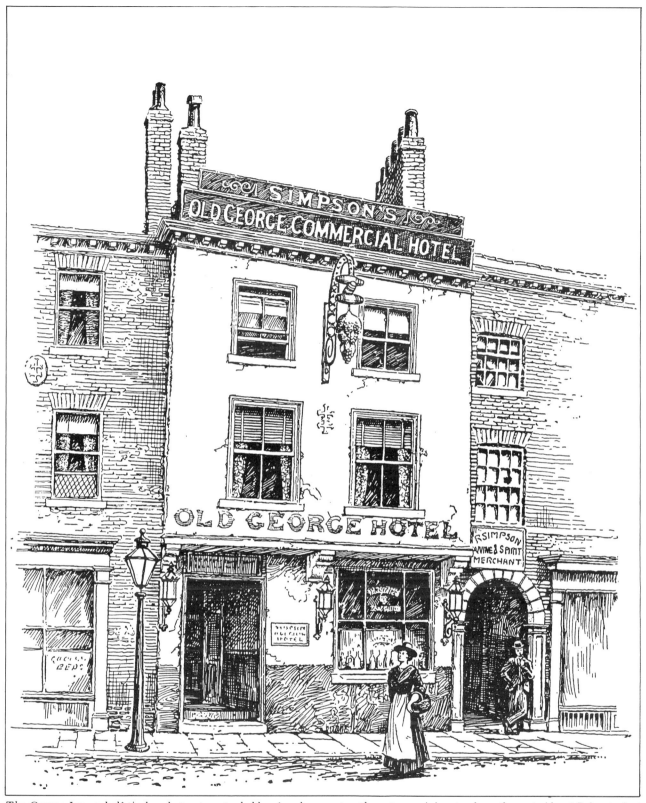

The George Inn, a half-timbered structure probably of early seventeenth-century origin, stood on the east side of Briggate just below the railway bridge, until its demolition around 1920. This drawing of the exterior of this coaching inn is by Percy Robinson, its interior being carefully observed in Charlotte Brontë's Jane Eyre *of 1847.*

a dinner given to O'Connell, and the Chartists having threatened an attack, Mr Marshall had a water-pipe under his chair which was supplied by a steam engine, and which he was ready to direct on the mob, if they had ventured to disturb him.

I spent one night here with Rev Wicksteed; one night with Mr Carbutt the Mayor, of whom Mrs Carbutt told me some excellent anecdotes; one night with George Hyde, Esq; and one with Joseph Lupton, Esq . . .

At Rawdon I inquired, how much the men earned who were breaking stone in the road, and was told twenty pence; but they can only have work three days in the week, unless they are married, then they can have it four days.

The Chartist, if you treat them civilly, and show any good will to their cause, suspect you, think you are going to *do* them.

1849

Angus Bethune Reach (1821-1856) began his career in investigative social journalism with the *Morning Chronicle* in 1842. As these evocative passages prove, he had an almost unqiue ability to re-create his personal observations in vivid prose. It is not surprising that this work has been described as 'an unparalleled exploit in journalism'.
Reach, A.B. 'Labour and the Poor' *The Morning Chronicle* 10 & 13 Dec.1849.

Leeds has little or none of that hot-house appearance which to some extent distinguishes Manchester. It seems in its physical peculiarities a more substantial and slower growing town than its high-pressure cotton neighbour, and it possesses none of the metropolitan attributes of the latter. Leeds has no public parks. With here and there an exceptional spot, the suburbs extend in mean, clumsy, straggling streets out into the bare country. There are no such fair ranges of villas as those which in many quarters skirt the busy portions of Manchester: and the dwellings of the labouring class, to which I shall speedily call attention, are, in point of appearance, and of symmetrical outward an convenient inward arrangement, decidedly inferior to those of the cotton capital . . .

I proceeded to the neighbouring row of cottages recently erected. These had each a common room, a bedroom, and a cellar loomshop. In the first when I entered, two Irishmen were weaving a coarse sacking, and the wife of one of them was winding in the bare, scarcely furnished room on the ground floor. The tenant of the room told me that the row was all alike, and belonged to the gentleman for whom he was working. The two looms were fixtures; of course, therefore, he could not rent them without renting the house. The rent was stopped every week out of his wages. Whatever they were, much or little, the rent must always come out of them before he got his money. He believed that the work was given to him just to enable him to pay the rent (which was 3s weekly), and thus to make a good return for the money invested in the house; otherwise it would be cheaper for the master to get the stuff woven by power. His wages, with his wife to wind, were very small, not averaging above 9s or 10s the highest. From another source I learnt that many of the poor weavers inhabiting houses built upon a similar plan, and with a similar view, had suffered most severely during the last season of depression. It often happened that their wages were entirely absorbed by the rent, while the parish refused them assistance on the very reasonable plea that a man who was paying 3s of weekly rent could not be said to be an object of charity. Thus these poor people had no means of obtaining work, except from a quarter which would give it to them, only on condition that they paid back all or the greater part of their remuneration in rent. In good times, of course, a weaver need not be so hard-driven; but if a master having work for ten men, and being also the landlord of ten houses, says to twenty men seeking employment, "I shall give my work to the ten who will consent to live in my ten houses, and pay me a high rent for them" then assuredly the scheme, if it does not actually amount to the truck system, is a very close imitation of it.

In all my peregrinations in the manufacturing capital of Yorkshire, I have not discovered a single operative dwelling with a back and front entrance, and consequently a through current of air. One man, indeed, said that he thought a double house were more whole some than single ones, because they were snugger and warmer: 'One heats the other,' he said, 'like sleeping two in a bed'. The illustration sums up the argument against the practice. In a large proportion of the

houses in question, the family, except when all are grown up, sleep together in the higher room. Beds in the lower room are, however, not uncommon. The furniture seldom shows the commonly existing neat comfort, or the less frequently occurring pretension, which marks Manchester tenements of different grades. A parlour kitchen can be made after its own fashion, a very cheerful apartment. Many a one I have recently visited, in which gleams of a good fire were playing on polished pot-lids and glancing crockery, arranged tidily and orderly upon the well-scoured racks, the floor either carpeted with a decent drugget, or nicely and trightly sanded: many a house of this class, I repeat, I have lately entered in which the sensation of comfort was very decidedly in the ascendant. But in Leeds I have found as a general rule domestic utensils coarser and scantier, and the spirit of neatness and good housewifery manifested on rarer occasions, and in a slighter degree . . .

The second and better class of houses, which form the minority, possess a sunken parlour kitchen, half the window of which only rises above the pavement. Above this apartment are placed two rooms in the ordinary manner. The sunken story is not quite a cellar and in many instances I found it dry, warm and cheerful. When it exists the ground floor room is very generally half unfurnished, the family making the lower apartment the ordinary living place. Good cooking-ranges are abundant. Water is seldom introduced into the houses; the stand-tap system being the usual one, each cook serving a greater or smaller number of houses according to the comparative poverty of the locality. The rents range for the medium class of dwellings, from 1s 6d to 3s weekly. The houses letting for the former sum are often old places, in bad repair, and with small close rooms. In almost every case the house door is the parlour door. Even in the very superior house, rented at 5s 6½d by the cloth weaver, a visit to which I have above described, there was no lobby, the door only separating the best room in the house from the street . . .

The corporation of Leeds, is I understand, about to spend a very large sum (about £30,000 or £40,000) in the formation of an extensive system of paving, drainage etc., in hitherto neglected portions of the borough. Never were sanitary reforms more imperatively called for. The condition of vast districts of the opulent and important town of Leeds is such that the very strongest language cannot overstate. Virulent and fatal as was the recent attack of cholera here, my wonder is that cholera, or some disease almost equally as fatal, is ever absent. From one house, for instance, situated in a large irregular court or yard — a small house containing two rooms — four corpses were recently carried. I looked about and did not marvel. The whole vicinage was two or three inches deep in filth. This seemed to be the normal state even of the passable parts of the place. In the centre of the open place was a cluster of pigsties, privies and cesspools, bursting with pent-up abominations; and a half a dozen paces from this delectable nucleus was a pit about five feet square filled to the very brim with semi-liquid manure gathered from stables and houses around. This yard lies on the south side of the Aire, not more than a gunshot from Leeds Bridge.

The east and north-east districts of Leeds are perhaps the worst. A short walk from the Briggate, in the direction in which Deansgate branches off from the main entry, will conduct the visitor into a perfect wilderness of foulness. Conceive acre on acre of little streets, run up without attention to plan or health — acre on acre of closely built and thickly peopled ground without a paving stone upon the surface, or an inch of sewer beneath, deep trodden — churned sloughs of mud forming the only thoroughfare — here and there an open space, used not exactly as a common cesspool, but the common cess-yard of the vicinity — in its centre, ash pits employed for dirtier purposes than containing ashes — privies, often ruinous, almost horribly foul — pig-sties very commonly left *protempore* untenanted, because their usual inmates have been turned out to prey upon the garbage of the neighbourhood. Conceive streets, and courts, and yards which a scavenger never appears to have entered since King John incorporated Leeds, and which gives the idea of a town built in a slimy bog. Conceive such a surface drenched with the liquid slops which each family flings out daily and nightly before their own threshold, and further fouled by the malpractices of children, for which the parents and not the children deserve shame and punishment. Conceive, in short, a whole district to which the above description truthfully and rigidly applies; and you will, I am sorry to say, have a fair idea of what at presents constitutes a large proportion of the operative part of Leeds.

I have seen here and there in Bradford spots very nearly, and in Halifax, spots quite as bad; but here it is no spot — the foulness over large sections of the town, particularly towards the suburbs, constitutes the very face and essence of things. I have plodded by the half hour through the streets in which the undisturbed mud lay in wreaths from wall to wall; and across open spaces, overlooked by houses all round, in which the pigs, wandering from this central oasis, seemed to be roaming through what was only a large sty. Indeed, pigs seem to be the natural inhabitants of such places. I think that they are more common in some parts of Leeds than dogs and cats are in others; and wherever they abound, wherever the population is the filthiest, there are the houses the smallest, the rooms the closest and the most overcrowded. One characteristic of such localities is a curious and significant one. Before almost every house-door there lies a little heap of boiled-out tea leaves, until of course, the pig comes upon the deposit. Although all the domestic refuse is flung out, you hardly ever see bones; but the teapot is evidently in operation at every meal. Here and there, I ought to add, the visitor will, even in the midst of such scenes as I have tried to sketch, come upon a cluster or a row of houses better than ordinary, and through the almost invariably open doors of which he will see some indications of domestic comfort; but such buildings are the exceptions — and exceptions as they are, they rise out of the same slough of mud and filth, and command the same ugly sights as their neighbours. There is I believe a Nuisance Committee in Leeds. I inquired whether they were aware of even the most flagrant of all these salutary enormities. Had their attention for instance, been ever drawn to the practice of keeping pigs, or rather letting pigs keep themselves in crowded neighbourhood?
"Yes", I was answered by a gentleman much interested in the subject, "yes, I have reported these things over and over again, until I was sick and tired of reporting; but you see nothing has been done".

It is to be hoped that Leeds is on the eve of a sanitary revolution, and that what is true of the town today will be but historic a twelve-month hence. Things are at present so palpably bad, that even a small outlay would make an immense change for the better. Even if it be impracticable to construct at once a thorough system of house sewerage, or to lay down at once miles of substantial paving, it would be surely easy, by means of the police, to compel the observance of something like ordinary human decency in the habits of children, to clean out and render available revolting cesspools, and to make a devastating razzia amongst those foul nuisances — in a crowded and often a fever-stricken locality — the pigs and pigsties.

I visited several cellars and wretched dwellings in the vicinity, inhabited by the Irish and the lowest class of English labourers, male and female, many of whom were engaged in the miserable occupation of unpicking old ropes, so as to prepare the oakum for being ground up again and wrought into shoddy, canvas and sacking. This special of labour is so unutterably wretched, that it can only exist as eking out the pittance procured by the industry of the principal supports of the family. The first woman upon whom I lighted, and who professed to follow this miserable trade, I found ill in bed. It was indeed a squalid household — the floor, dirty stone — the mean furniture scanty and broken — the smashed window panes stuffed with rags — and an emaciated woman, ghastly as death, lying shivering on a flock bed on the floor covered principally with a dress and a faded shawl. She told me that she could earn just 4d by unpicking a stone of just ordinary ropes, and that she was too weak to pick more than three stone a week. The family lived principally on parish relief. She did not mean to say that a better hand than she was could not make more by opening ropes. She could not work at it longer than from eight o'clock in the morning until four o'clock in the afternoon. It was terribly dusty work. The house would be all covered with dust. The labour was awfully hard upon the fingers, particularly with the ropes were "green". For this kind of work however she was paid a penny a stone additional.

I was anxious to see the process actually going on, and presently I came upon a household in which, poor as were its physical attributes, the moral debasement and apathy which it disclosed were still more terrible. In a bare, stone-paved room, a principal part of the furniture of which consisted of tubs and apparatus for washing, sat three young children, cowering over a spark of fire, and slowly and painfully tearing rough ropes to pieces with their weak bony little fingers. An intelligent girl, about eight or nine years of age, seemed to have the control of the other children, who were younger and for whom she spoke, labouring away all the time. I ought to observe that I was accompanied by a relieving officer, and that the father of the family had been receiving parish relief for seven years.

"Where's your mother?" — "Gone out to try and get some washing to do".
"Where's your father?" — "In the Fleece — that's a public house. Ah! mother told him that he had better not go today, for you (to the releiving officer) would be very likely to come round; but he wouldn't stay".
"What does your father do? — "Sweeps the streets sometimes".
"But does he not help you pick these ropes?" — "No; he wouldn't do that. He makes *us* do that".
"What do you get for picking?" — "Fourpence a stone but I give it all to my mother".
"Do you go to school?" — "Only on Sundays. I must work you know. I can't read yet. But my little brother goes to school on week-days. Parson pays for him: only sometimes they keeps him at home to help in picking. He can't read either".
"And is not the other little boy your brother?" — "Oh no! He only comes in to help us pick".
"Do you like picking?" — "No, because it makes me poorly. The dust gets into my eyes and down my throat, and makes me cough. Sometimes too, it makes me sick. I can't keep at the work very long at a time, because of that".
"You say you give all you earn to your mother?" — "Does she never let you have a penny for yourself?"

The poor child hung down her head, hesitated and then stammered out, "sometimes".

"And what do you do with it?" "I buys bread".

In another house, very close to the last, I found three children left alone but in idleness. The place was a mess of filth; the scanty furniture broken, and flung carelessly about — the unmade bed a chaos of brown rags — cracked and handleless cups, smeared with coffee grounds, on the floor, amid unemptied slops and beside a large brown dish, full of fermenting dough, upon which dust and ashes were rapidly settling as it stood at the fireside. The uncleaned window and the dim light of a winter's afternoon made the place so dark that it was with difficulty I made out these details. There were here three little savages of children — their hair tangled in filthy, clotted masses hanging over their grimy faces. Their clothes were mere bunches of rags, kept together by strings. A wriggle of their shoulders, and they would be free from all such incumbrances in a moment.

I asked them if they ever went to school? — "Never". "Can you tell your letters?" — A mere solid stare of ignorance. "How old are you?" I asked the eldest girl — "Don't know." "Do you know what is the Queen's name?" — "No". "Where were you born" — "Don't know." The relieving officer said that he believed all the family were Irish. "Did you ever hear of a place called Ireland?" — "No." "Or of a place called England?" — "No". "Or of a place called Yorkshire?" — "No". "Do you know the name of this town?"

After a pause, the question was answered. The eldest girl did know she lived in Leeds; and this knowledge, with the exception of matters belonging to the daily routine of existence, seemed positively to be the only piece of information in the possession of the family . . .

I visited the only two slop-workers I could hear of. One was receiving public charity; the other was a wife of a weaver, who stated that he earned 17s a week. The former made in substance the following statement. She laboured in fustian and corduroy trousers, working jackets and working sleeved waistcoats. All these garments were lined with cotton. For making a pair of trousers she had 10d, and her thread found her. She could make a pair in a day. By a day she meant from seven o'clock in the morning till ten o'clock at night. For lined jackets and sleeved waistcoats she used to get 15d each, but the price had been reduced lately. Sometimes she made drawers for which she was paid 4d a pair. They had buttons and button holes all complete. Work as she might, she could not finish two pair in a day, and the utmost she could make in a week, with the very hardest labour, was 5s. The second slop-worker was principally employed on boys' dresses. These she made in three sorts and sizes, the first and smallest size consisting of a jacket and trousers, the latter buttoning over the former. For such a suit, generally of corduroy, she received 1s 4d, and she could make one in a day. The second class suit consisted of a jacket, trousers and waistcoat. For this she was paid 2s 6d and to make it took a good day and a half. The third class suit consisted of a surtout with skirts, a waistcoat and a jacket. For this she was paid 3s 6d, and she took more than two days to earn it. These were the main articles of a dress which she sewed, and she cut them out herself. She sometimes, however, made moleskin jackets and waistcoats such as are worn by engineers. These, from the nature of the stuff, are very hard work. For a waistcoat of this kind with sleeves, she was paid 1s 3d. For a double-breasted waistcoat, without sleeves she was paid 9d. Her hours of work were from seven in the morning until ten, eleven, twelve o'clock as the case might be. She found her own thread. In all the garments which she made she put regular lining.

c **1850**

This broadside ballad is undated, but was probably written around 1850 It most likely refers to Woodhouse Lane, then frequented by people walking to and from Woodhouse Moor for their Sunday stroll, together with soldiers from the Cavalry Barracks at Sheepscar and those 'Naughty girls from Regent Street'.

Sunday Night
I'm about to sing a stunning song;
And yet the subject it's not long,
It's all about the funny sights —
In -----Lane on a Sunday Night
One half of the people of (Leeds) be near,
Between four and ten are walking there,
All other walks are deserted quite,
For -----Lane on a Sunday Night.
Chorus
If you doubt the truth of what I say,
And wish to prove it in my way;
Now go yourself and take a sight.
in -----Lane on a Sunday Night.

Old Batchelors they are strutting away,
Laughing and chaffing with maidens gay,
And sour old maids too there you'll find,
With their little pet dogs trotting behind
And soldiers in red coats so gay
With Factory lasses are marching away,
Bragging of how they can sing and fight —
In -----Lane on a Sunday Night.

If you doubt &c.

To take a walk I do declare,
All men and women do repair,
Smart young fellows dressed up so grand,
With a cut away coat and stick in hand;
And servant lasses fat and plump,
With a great big bustle on their rump,
Rambling out in great delight
Along the road on Sunday Night.

Above the barracks there you will meet,
With naughty girls from Regent Street.
Who up to your elbows close will steer,
And whisper softly 'good night my dear'
And if with them you dare to stop,
They'll gammon you to stand a drop,
And they'll diddle you out of your cash
    all right,
Is -----Lane on a Sunday Night.

Young widows tired of a single life,
Each wanting again to become a wife,
Are trying with many a wicked lady,
To catch a swellish husband dear.
And handsome fellows are pushing along
    singing,
'That licks me', or some such song:
With sweethearts under their arm all right
How loving they are on Sunday Night.

These loving couples each other meet;
Dress'd up in Sunday clothes so neat,
Calling each other dears and loves,
Billing and cooing like turtle doves;

And under shadow of the trees lawk,
How they does each other squeeze,
If those trees could speak what tales they
   would tell,
Of -----Lane on a Sunday night.

But the sight that me the most annoys,
Is to see so many little boys,
Who instead of being with their mamas,
Are strutting about there smoking cigars,
And girls not seventeen years old,
A courting and sporting with them,
And doing of that what is not right,
In -----Lane on a Sunday night.

Now an incident I'll tell to you,
Which proves this verse to be true,
It's what a mother was heard to say,
When her daughter was in a particular way
The mother when viewing her daughter's
   size exclaimd,
As tears stood in her eyes,
Oh! you hussy how came you in that plight,
"If you please ma," it happened —
In -----Lane one Sunday night.

Now to conclude and make an end,
With these few verses I have penn'd,
Come all you pretty damsels gay,
A warning take by what I say,
For if with young men you should go,
And they should prove your overthrow,
Your waist will swell & stays grow tight,
By rambling out on Sunday night.

1857

William Osburn (1793-1875), son of a Leeds wine-merchant, was a prominent Egyptologist, taking a leading part in the unwrapping of Leeds Museum's mummy of the Egyptian priest Natsef Amun, and going on to write a number of popular books on this subject. Here, however, he likens the state of the River Aire to the Styx, the dark river of the Greek underworld, across which the souls of the dead were ferried by Charon.
Osburn, W.
(A poem read before members of the Leeds Philosophical and Literary Society 1857).

"The AIRE below is doubly dyed and damned;
The AIR above, with lurid smoke is crammed;
The ONE flows steaming foul as Charon's Styx,
Its poisonous vapours in the other mix.
These sable twins the murky town invest-
By them the skin's begrimed, the lungs oppressed.
How dear the penalty thus paid for wealth;
Obtained through wasted life and broken health;
The joyful Sabbath comes! that blessed day,
When all seem happy, and when all seen gay!
Then toil has ceased, and then both rich and poor
Fly off to Harrogate or Woodhouse Moor.
The one his villa and a carriage keeps;
His squalid brother in a garret sleeps,
HIGH flaunting forest trees, LCW crouching weeds,
Can this be Manchester? or is it Leeds?"

1857

Charles Dickens (1812-1870), the author of those great Victorian classics *Pickwick, Oliver Twist, Nicholas Nickleby* etc, visited Leeds on a number of occasions, when he enthralled great audiences with his famous dramatic readings. Even so, his opinion of the town was far from complimentary.
Dexter, W. *The England of Dickens* (1925) p.231
   Leeds has changed wondrously since Idle and Goodchild arrived at the station with "a little rotten platform (converted into artifical touchwood by smoke and ashes)" by way of the "branchless wood of vague black chimneys . . .of the manufacturing bosom of Yorkshire". The great manufacturing towns "looked in the cinderous wet, as though they had one and all been on fire and were just put out".
   Of the "enterprising and important centre of Leeds," Dickens remarked that "it may be observed with delicacy that you must either like it very much or not at all". And he emphasised his dislike of Leeds in a letter to Miss Hogarth from Lancaster on 12 September, 1857, when, proposing to go to Doncaster on the following day (Sunday) he wrote that he found the trains so inconvenient that he feared he would have to sleep the night at Leeds, "which I particularly detest as an odious place".

1858

This broadside song was probably sold around the densely crowded streets of Leeds during Victoria and Albert's visit in September 1858.

A NEW SONG ON THE
QUEEN'S VISIT TO LEEDS

Come all good people high and low,
And listen to my song,
I'll sing a merry ditty,
And will not detain you long;
It's concerning the Queen's visit,
To the town of Leeds so gay,
And may all classes, high and low,
Enjoy that glorious day.

Chorus
So we'll shout and sing, God save the Queen
And may her reign be long;
And cheer the worthy Mayor of Leeds,
As they do pass along.

From all the neighbouring towns around
Many thousands they will go,
From York, from Bradford, Halifax,
And Huddersfield also;
From Shefield, Wakefield, Pontefract,
In merry droves they're seen,
Shouting with voices loud and long,
God bless our gracious Queen.

Come all you tradesmen now of Leeds,
Begin for to prepare,
To greet the Queen so welcome,
Follow the example of the Mayor
Prepare your illuminations,
With flags and banners gay,
And let everything be ready,
By that long expected day.

This wood engraving from the Illustrated London News *shows the arrival of Queen Victoria and Prince Albert at the steps of Leeds Town Hall on 7 September 1858. A short time later, from the platform of the crowded Victoria Hall, she declared this magnificent building open.*

Old Leeds with flags and banners,
And triumphal green,
Upon that day it will look gay,
To welcome England's Queen;
The merry lads and lasses fair,
Each other they will jostle,
I say there Bill, just stop that girl,
I declare she's dropp'd her bustle.

In the Briggate as I pass'd along,
I heard an old woman way
That she would have a grand flare-up
Upon that glorious day;
With red, white & blue, her bonnet's trim'd,
She means to but it fine,
For she's got a skirt with hoops inside,
which they call crinoline.

To see the thousands of spectators,
Round about the New Town Hall,
Butchers, bakers, hotel-waiters,
Tinkers, tailors, snobs and all;
Children pouting, women shouting,
To see the sight they all do run,
Some are busy picking pockets,
Some do take them as they come.

Guns a firing, bells a ringing,
Boys and girls all dress'd so gay,
Here she comes! cries one; now for it,
Let her hear us shout hurrah!
I saw a lass call'd Sally Petty,
Run like twinkling thro' the town,

For she diddled a country booby,
Our of his watch and half-a-crown.

So to conclude and end my song,
I hope you will not frown,
But young lasses, don't let the young men
Rumble the flounces of your gown;
For if you do you're sure to rue,
And a babe you'll have I ween,
To keep you in remembrance of,
The visit of the Queen.

J.Bebbington, Printer, 31 Oldham Road, Manchester, Sold by J.Beaumont, 176 York Street, Leeds.

1858

Dickens, C.
The letters of Charles Dickens (1880) p.72-3.
Miss Dickens

SCARBOROUGH ARMS, LEEDS, Wednesday, 15 September 1858.

MY DEAREST MAMIE,
    Since I wrote to Georgy from Scarborough, we have had, thank God, nothing but success. This place I have always doubted, knowing that we should come here when it was recovering from the double excitement of the festival and the Queen. But there is a very large hall let indeed, and the prospect of to-night consequently looks bright . . .
    Oddly enough, I slept in this house three days last year

Since over two hundred years had elapsed since a reigning English sovereign had come to Leeds, the whole town made every effort to celebrate Victoria and Albert's visit in the most lavish manner. This delightfully naive lithograph shows them passing down Briggate beneath a tremendous show of bunting, flags and other patriotic decorations.

with Wilkie. Arthur has the bedroom I occupied then, and I have one two doors from it, and Gordon has the one between . . .

These streets look like a great circus with the season just finished. All sorts of garish triumphal arches were put up for the Queen, and they have got smoky, and have been looked out of countenance by the sun, and are blistered and patchy, and half up and half down, and are hideous to behold. Spiritless men (evidently drunk for some time in the royal honour) are slowly removing them, and on the whole it is more like the clearing away of 'The Frozen Deep' at Tavistock House than anything within your knowledge — with the exception that we are not in the least sorry, as we were then. Vague ideas are in Arthur's head that when we come back to Hull, we are to come here, and are to have the Town Hall (a beautiful building), and read to the million. I can't say yet. That depends. I remember that when I was here before (I came from Rockingham to make a speech), I thought them a dull and slow audience. I hope I may have been mistaken. I never saw better audiences than the Yorkshire audiences generally.

1859

Walter White (1811-1893) tried cabinet-making and clerical work before becoming 'attendant' at the library of the Royal Society in 1844, and then its assistant secretary and librarian in 1861. It was here that he started his serious literary work, and made a number of holiday walks to furnish material for his numerous books.
White, W. *A Month in Yorkshire* 1859 p.266.

'I travelled by rail to Leeds. I had little time, and, remembering former days, less inclination to tarry in this great, dismal cloth-weaving town; so after a passing glance at the new town-hall, and some other improvements, I walked through the long, scraggy suburb such as only a busy manufacturing town can create, to Kirkstall Abbey (which) stands only a few yard from a black, much-frequented road, and within sight and hearing of a big forge . . . I had expected to see the valley of the Aire sprinkled with the villa residences of the merchants of Leeds; but the busy traders prefer to live in town, and in all the nine miles on the way to Bradford, you have only a succession of factories, dye-works, and excavations, encroaching on and deforming the beauty of the valley, while the vegetation betrays signs of the harmful effect of smoke . . . so I turned aside to Newlay station, and took flight by the first train that came up for Settle.

1865

John Thomlinson was chiefly a local historian and topographical writer about the Doncaster area, but his guides to Ben Rhydding and Bolton Abbey, and accounts of interesting Yorkshire scenes published in the mid 1860s, contain a wealth of closely-observed detail.
Thomlinson, J. *Some Interesting Yorkshire Scenes* (1865) p.15 and 29.

I turned out of Upperhead-row into Briggate, and was soon hemmed in amongst the crowd; not unobservant, however, of what was passing around. Immediately in front was a trio of elegantly dressed nymphs, whose expansive crinoline subjected both themselves and others to considerable annoyance. The pavement, as before mentioned, is broad; but these ladies' skirts could not be less than five feet in diameter; three times five are fifteen; now, without wishing to interfere unnecessarily with the liberty of the subject, I cannot but think that fifteen feet of public causeway ought not to be appropriated by three individuals. Granting that steel or whalebone is a desirable protection from the jostling of the baser sex, still, when two or three ladies walk out together in the public thoroughfares on busy occasions, they should, at least, range themselves in single file, and as closely as possible, like policemen on drill.

In passing the cab stand, which extends from the top of Briggate to the corner of Commercial-street, I made two observations — first, that the quality of the vehicles was far superior to the value of the horses, and secondly, that the

latter appear to enjoy but an indifferent lot. Grave and bending with years or infirmities, many of the dumb creatures seemed to have acquired a tinge of melancholy.

I afterwards found on looking in at two other very central, and even commercial hotels, that the plan of evening singing-rooms was exceedingly popular in Leeds. That the scheme pays is quite evident, as well from the number of people which one meets at those places, as from the fact that nothing but large profits would induce landlords of old respectable inns to hire female singers, and thus entice together shoals of young clerks and tradesmen's gay assistants.

There were brilliant lights streaming from a gin-shop near the top of Briggate, while sounds of merriment echoed from the half-open door. I debated within myself whether or not I should see what was going on. Propriety said — It is not right to enter those places, for by so doing you are countenancing a great social evil. Not so, another voice replied to the monitor, for how can I appreciate my duty to those erring fellow-creatures, until I have witnessed their degradation? Immediately behind the door was stationed a harper and a fiddler, with their instruments lying carelessly beside them, while they partook of rum-and-water, hot, which had been paid for by one of the fast young gents in the company. I called for a glass of sherry. By my side was a nervous, modest-looking young man, whose eyes sparkled too brilliantly as he sipped his glass in silence. Ranged along the counter were five or six nymphs, some with very pink cheeks, other with very black lustrous eyes, and all gaudily if not expensively dressed. One of them shewed a disposition to be on affable and familiar terms with the youth alluded to, enquiring in a very bewitching manner — "Well, my dear, and how are you to-night"?

1869

Tommy Toddles' 'Comic Almenac for all 't'Foaks e Leeds, nut furgettin them at Hunslet Moarsoide, Howlbeck Spaws an Woodus Ridge' was first published by J.Hamer of Briggate in 1862, and continued annually up to 1875. Each edition gives details of events in the town written in a broad Yorkshire dialect.
Tommy Toddles' Leeds Almenac, 1869.
(a visit to the 1868 National Exhibition of Works of Art, Leeds Infirmary).

Well now, you'll happen think that I'm nobbut a gawky, because I live among the cherry-trees at Rawdon, but choose how it is, I mean to tell you about my visit to the Leeds Exhibition and all I saw there . . .
At Leeds, we had to begin and ask the way to the Exhibition. We thought we were fools for asking, when we saw a big board up on a pillar, with "This way to the Exhibition" on, and the shape of a man's hand pointing. Says I to myself, "We're much obliged to the bill-sticker, I'm sure; he must have known we were coming"; and up the steps we went, and I asked, for Sally and me, if we could see the pictures, if they pleased. The great fat fellow that we asked took off his eye-glass to have a look at us, and he began laughing. "See the pictures!" said he, there's no pictures here, my man; we're all living examples, and most of us reading the newspapers" (they had entered the commercial buildings). Well, we found our way down into the street again, with Sally feeling mad instead of ashamed; but that's her way of being shamed, as she never feels nothing that doesn't show; she turned back to shake her fist in that impudent chap's face, and then went with me comforted. Before we got far we saw a policeman, and he took us right to the place, and

Despite the widening of streets such as Boar Lane, seen here at its junction with Briggate, they were still extremely congested as horse-drawn trams, delivery waggons and hansom cabs fought their way through crowds of shoppers workers and numerous street-traders. In such circumstances, large crinoline dresses were decidedly anti-social.

we paid our brass and got in, through a turnabout, something like the old one at Calverley Var, but that it went click, click, click and click again, before we got beyond . . .

. . .We went forwards, and got into a long passage, with all makes of likenesses hanging up against the wall sides. They were all called the Yorkshire Worthies, I told her, there were all the preachers there that had been born in Yorkshire since Adam died. Then we took along another passage, and lit on a chap like a butcher, with braiding of red round his cap, and I stopped him and told him we wanted to see the main things by good daylight, and asked him to show us the places to go to. He says, "Then you'd better go to the Britishers, living and deceased. There's some painting in oil there, mind you". "Painted with oil", said Sally, when she'd got in to them, "What will they make of us next? them's painted with paint!", and she shook her fist at the chap as he was going away again. We stopped at the "Death of Chatterton", and when I told Sally about him, she said she liked John Wesley herself, meaning that she liked poetry. Then she looked and said "Poor lad!" and gave a great fetch of breath, as if she had found out she's no meal for next baking day.

When we'd almost got all seen there we heard a band strike up, and as Sally's fearful fond of music, we made our way and listened to it. They said it was a German band, did some chaps in billycocks and straw bengies that were there; and to be sure if there's any brass to pick up in the music line and foreigners manage it, generally. After the music was over we jogged on a bit, and got into another hole full of nothing but pictures, and right stalled we were of seeing them. Then we found ourselves in an old curiosity shop, and Sally was fairly bewildered, and said we should never get to see half of what there was to see, not if we stopped for a month. She said she felt faint, and her feet ached about the ankles more than a bit. I told her to try and get herself a cup of tea if she could, and as for me,

don't mention it, I'd pay my respects to the oven-cakes and my taste of pig.

We went into a place where there was something set out to eat, and sat ourselves down to rest us. There were a lot of folk sitting at little tables, most of them with bits of ham and bread before them that would weight about half an ounce, and cost thruppence. I felt chuff that I'd got my pocket so well trigged, and started pulling my cakes out, when Lo and behold! a lot of white handkerchiefed chaps came up, and said I wasn't to eat nothing there, "This is a bonny state of things" said I to Sally, "there'll be a rising and Revolution next".

*c.*1870

This broadside ballad was sung to the tune of the well-known song *Vilikens and Dinah*. It probably enjoyed great popularity in the pubs of Victorian Leeds, where the pleasures and risks of the Dark Arches were well known.

Down by the Dark Arches
(Broadside Ballad to the tune of 'Vilikens & Dinah)

As I walked out one day in the month of July
A pretty young damsel I chanced for to spy,
Singing Vilikens and Dinah, so blithe and so gay,
Down by the dark arches under the railway.

Then I stepped up to her so gay and so free,
And for the same ballad I paid one halfpenny,
Will you be my sweetheart to her I did say,
Down by the dark arches under the railway.

Oh no, my gay young man that cannot be,
There is a chap here in blue and he is a-watching of me,
And if he should see me, what would he say,
Down by the dark arches under the railway.

Between 1846 and 1869 a series of enormous railway viaducts were built between the town centre and the river in order to provide a high-level route across the busy streets. Some of the 'Dark Arches' beneath the railway were used as warehouses and workshops, while others, particularly those close to the Leeds and Liverpool Canal docks, were frequented by 'Ladies of the Night'. As this ballad confirmed, the young men who came here for a good time could get far more than they bargained for!

At last she consented, away we both went,
Five shillings in lobsters and oysters I spent,
Six drops of brandy for her I did pay,
Down by the dark arches under the railway.

Then in came a chap with a black eye and a stick,
He drunk up my brandy and broke my Pickwick;
Pop goes the weasel to me he did say,
Down by the dark arches under the railway.

Then he squared up to me and pulled my watch out,
He spoiled my new beaver and damaged my snout,
He kicked me in the gutter and there I lay,
Down by the dark arches under the railway.

I lay in the gutter till four in the morn
As naked as ever a poor creature was born,
And when I awakened quite still there I lay,
Down by the dark arches under the railway.

Four bobbies came up and to my surprise
I found I had no shirt on to cover my thighs,
They put me on a stretcher and bore me away
From beneath the dark arches under the railway.

I sent to my mother for money and clothes,

Likewise to a doctor to patch up my nose,
You have not had fair play to me he did say
Down by the dark arches under the railway.

Now all you young chaps take a warning by me,
And never go a-courting when you are on the spree,
And never take those young ladies out of their way
Down by the dark arches under the railway.

*c.*1870

Henry Marles was a local preacher and romantic poet, publishing volumes such as *Kirkstall Abbey, Adel uburn, or the Fickleness of Fortune,* and *Wild Flowers from the Wayside of Life.* Although these are seldom read today, they do contain works which reflect the concerns and attitudes of many of the inhabitants of Victorian Leeds.
Marles, H. *A Sanctuary for the Afflicted* (Leeds).

'Being a poem on the Leeds General Infirmary'
Upon a sloping ground a temple rose,
Deem'd with propriety, the fane of health;
To its erection there were found no foes,
Yet did its rise exhaust a mine of wealth . . .
The faulty were all of standing high,
Men whom their fellows could with safety trust;

The General Infirmary at Leeds moved into these magnificent purpose-built premises in 1868. Designed by George Gilbert Scott, with advice from Florence Nightingale, it represented the very highest standards of modern hospital design, and improved levels of care for its patients.

So that the weary sufferer could rely,
And have no secret feelings of disgust . . .
The nurses next — a trichord strong and grand —
Moved as the faculty would have them move;
Self-acting, yet obedient to command,
With hands almost as soft as hands of love . . .
Severe in its simplicity — the place
In all that ministers to health abounds —
And cleanliness itself, must wash its face,
Or be detected in these magic grounds,
Surgeons and nurses passing through their rounds,
With glance as keen as fires the eagle's sight,
Correct each fault-evil each hand impounds,
Yet not with frowns are all kept acting right,
Kindness has laws more potent, and more
blest and bright . . .

c.**1870**

F.M.Fetherston's character 'Timothy Goorkrodger' was a bluff Yorkshire farmer who visited a wide variety of interesting locations with his Dame, his daughter Mary, and occasionally his 'Scapegrace Nevvy'. They always made the most of these excursions, and expressed their views in full-blooded Yorkshire dialect.
Fetherston, F.M. *Ooops and Doons . . .of Timothy Goorkrodger* . . . (Huddersfield) 76-86.

The chief street of Leeds is called Briggate. It's a long up-hill road with houses of all shapes and sizes; some are grand, some tumble-down, some with pointed roofs, some with flat ones, some lanky, some broad, some cottage-like, some palaces — giants and dwarfs, old and new fashioned, white, red, grey, black, but almost all with noble and bonny shows of goods in the windows, with everything a man can want, for the inside and the outside, and enough and to spare.

There's a new street, Boar Lane they've called it, by Briggate, though it's no more like a lane than I look like

a taylor. There are some splendid shops there, I think that lane beats any street or gate in Leeds; and if they go on so, and make such lanes, I wonder, bigow, what their best streets will be some day!

. . .then we made for the Town Hall. At Bonnybeck, we've a pretty picture of it in colours; it was given away with some illustrated newspaper in London, I believe. It's a light yellow, in sunshine, with blue sky overhead, and trees and bushes behind. But the light yellow is sooty black, the blue sky is black with clouds of smoke, and the trees and bushes are two miles off. But that Town Hall is really a fine place, though there's muck enough on it to take all the chimney sweeps of Leeds a week to clean it. For all that, it's a grand building, and must have cost a mint of brass. We mounted up some broad, long steps, twenty or more, I think, with great lions at each end, and went under the pillars, ever so high above your head, into the hall. And I can tell all my Yorkshire friends it's well worth seeing is that same inside, if they take some trouble and a bit of a journey to come. All the ceiling is gold and colours, and marble pillars, with arches of bright shiny stuff, and glass candlesticks above for lights. They've got images of Baines and Rob Hall inside . . .there's seats and chairs by thousands, and a monster of an organ which would make twenty of our Bonnybeck church organs right out, I know.

Well, the Dame and Mary and I sat down, with hundreds of others, to hear Doctor Sparke and Tommy Dodd play; though why a doctor should play the organ, I don't know; if he physics and looks after men's organs as well as he *plays* on that organ, he must cure many! Tommy Dodd is so well liked in Leeds, the bairns have got a song about him,
"Heads or tails he's sure to win,
Tommy Dodd, Tommy Dodd!"

They did play beautifully, and folk clapped their hands, and I clapped my hands, and knocked with my big stick, till a man sitting near said "Don't knock a hole in the floor, my friend," and I coloured up, and stopped. Next a young lady came forward and sang like a nightingale . . .How we all clapped and shouted till we made her come and show her pretty face again! Then a man sung another piece about "Other lips and other hearts", and "tales of love", and a lot more like that, and it seemed to please all the young folk amazingly, but I liked better another piece by the same man . . .and when I left the Town Hall, I felt better for hearing that music and those songs, I did.

I think the people of Leeds are doing right; their fine Town Hall could not be better made use of, and I hope they'll go on, and give the Leeds working folk and others every chance of leaving drink, and spending their time in such places. Put Town Hall Concerts against Public House Concerts, with their dirt, and noise, and beastliness, and my word I know which will conquer in the long run.

In the words of the bairns, I say "Success to Tommy Dodd (and Dr Sparke too); he's sure to win the day!". And so *"good bye"* to smoky Leeds till I write another book'

1872

Charles Kirby (1943-?), 'the Wharfedale Poet' spent most of his youth as a cattle-boy and as a joiner, spending only short periods at Tadcaster Grammar School. His poetry received considerable local encouragement, however, and a number of volumes of his works appeared in print.
Kirby, C. *The Struggle and Victory* (Leeds 1872) p.1

THE APPEAL
Oh, men of Leeds! oh, men of station high!
We ask the priceless privilege to breathe;
Our throats and sluggish lungs are nearly choked
With smoke and gas; our eyes with dust and glare
Are dim; our ears, with noise from rumbling wheels
And cranks and hammers' sounds, are growing dull:
From polluted streams, and dark and dreary
Courts, and closed-up dens, we ask in pity
For the privilege to breathe! For we are
Weary grown, and faint, and sick at heart: Our
Children's cheeks, once so fair, now pale and wan, call
For space to breathe! From our muscles, bone, and
Brain, your gold is much drived. We envy
Not your pleasures not the luxuries it brings:
Ah, no! we wish you health and every joy
That gardens gay and beauteous houses give:
But, while enjoying, ah, remember us!
Though working men, do we not souls possess,
And bodies formed of self-same flesh and blood
As you? In the name of God, fellow mortals,
We urge our claim for space — pure air to breathe!

c.1879

Richard Barr was a Leeds book-seller, printer, newsagent and tobacconist, who published many broadsides, ballad sheets etc. from his successive shops in Marsh Lane, Bridge Street and York Street. This poem celebrates the beauties of the recently-opened Roundhay Park.
Barr, R. *Roundhay Park*

Riding to Roundhay then a walk in the Park,
Over the stepping-stones then thro' the park
Under the Trees, a seat in the shade:
Neared to the Mansion, a rest in the Glade.
Dancing and singing, Music that's Free.
Here is refreshments, ham, cake and tea!
And I must away to see the writing-on-glass
Yes, Castle Hermitage, and Boat-house, at last.

Please keep on the walks, no damage do?
A beautiful Park, what a grand view!
Roundhay-road, what a dust and smother,
Keep order and you may come again to-morrow.
The Ivy Tower, 51 steps
By, Leeds Richard.

1893

Tom Bradley was a Yorkshire sporting writer who produced a number of popular guides to cycling, fishing and coaching in the county during the 1890s. They all have a lively style and make interesting reading. The following passages first appeared in the pages of *The Yorkshire Weekly Post*.
Bradley, T. *Yorkshire Rivers, No.9 Part 1. The Aire* (Leeds 1893) 29-36.

Approaching Knostrop we meet one of the first monuments of the sublime superiority of the Leeds Corporation, namely Knostrop Sewage Works. This establishment, we are told, purifies the sewage of the town, extracts from it all that is vile and noisome, and turns it out pure as a silvery rill, dancing o'er its mossy bed, in order not to pollute the sweet, pellucid Aire. Such an effort at high-souled purity is a noble enterprise on the part of any Corporation; but there must have something gone wrong with the works on the day we happened to be there, for this outlet of purity to the river was a vile, floating, coagulated mass of stinking impurity.

Should anyone doubt the fact that we have arrived within the borough of Leeds, let him look at the mud which embellishes his patent leathers, the blacks that have settled on his erstwhile white cravat, and the halo of grime which surrounds his classical features — all of which bear the trade-mark of Hunslet — and he will breath a silent and poetic conviction in language that he durst not use before his mother-in-law, that "this is indeed Leeds" . . .

Leeds can hardly be termed a picturesque city, though some one once suggested that it was a place an artist might revel in. This was many years ago. The artist that could revel in Leeds now could revel in anything. Still we are told it has its picturesque corners. Fancy the touching landscapes of Lady Lane, sandy Lobby, and the Isle of Cinder. These historic districts have never yet had justice done them on the painter's canvas. Much of Leeds wants painting; it wants painting badly . . .

Take Briggate, for instance — one of the finest streets possessed by any town in England. This, being the principal

street of Leeds, should embrace some of its best features. What have we instead? A strange mixture of shops and buildings embracing all the styles in Christendom, besides a few that cannot claim parentage, without one solitary structure of any architectural pretensions from end to end . . .The styles in Briggate belong to a great extent to the tinpot and gimcrack order of architecture, and they bear a strong affinity to the majority of the chief individual structures throughout the town . . .the late Lord Beaconsfield once said that it would do good to hang an architect occasionally, as terror has its inspiration as well as competition.

Our business is with the River Aire as it wanders through the town, rather than with the town itself . . .In its lazy, sluggish fashion, the dark and dirty Aire of today drags its course through the centre of the town, a putrid bed of filthy excrement . . .where thousands of people daily pass and are obliged to breathe its fever-laden vapours. We wonder how many people of the vast number who every day use the two stations in the centre of the town know that they are built over the noisome River Aire. Yet in the hot summer time the stream asserts itself; at times the stench is unendurable, and although the stream is unseen it is always too much in evidence unless there has something gone wrong with one's nasal organ.

1894

Edited by Albert T.Marles, *Hypnotic Leeds* contained a number of essays on the social condition of the city. This extract was written by Joseph Clayton, who is described in the local directories as a blanket-raiser of 9 Longwood Terrace, Hunslet.
Marles, A.T. 'Housing of the Poor' *Hypnotic Leeds* (Leeds, 1894).

The typical workman's house in Leeds has one living room, adorned with sink and taps for washing purposes, two bedrooms, and an attic in which possibly is a bath. The bath is the one redeeming point, and the corporation should insist on it being built in every house.

The sinks and taps on the other hand are depressing in a sitting-room, and the smell of the atmosphere of the weekly wash not conducive to health of mind or body. If we prefer to dry our clothes across the street and not indoors we may gratify our neighbours' curiosity as to the condition and quality of our under-clothing, but the smoke of Leeds resents our brandishing clean clothes in the open air and showers down smuts. Of the necessary sanitary arrangements of every dwelling-house — it is difficult to speak calmly in Leeds. Our ashpits which adorn the street are the resting place for decayed vegetable matter, and domestic refuse generally; the stench from them is probably a sweet smelling savour to the arch-fiend, but it is poison to the children who play around them.

The worst of it is these houses with their ashpits, etc., are still being built — in the face of all our sanitary knowledge — and no one protests . . .

Notwithstanding that medical reports have pronounced vehemently against back-to-back houses, and that in some large towns — Manchester being one of them — their erection has been prohibited, yet in Leeds the jerry builder flourishes, crushing into a small space rows of these red brick kennels. It was not until 1886 that a separate account of the different classes of houses was kept in Leeds, but during the twelve years ending August 1887, 16,070 new houses of all classes built were certified as fit for habitation; and of these it was estimated that at least two-thirds were back-to-back. In the six years following, out of 7,333 houses built, no fewer than 4,959 were of the back-to-back class. In 1889-90 nearly 1,200 were erected, and still the game goes on. A motion made in the City Council to prohibit the building of such houses met with a crushing defeat which was to be expected from a body of which most of the members are property owners.

1896

Robert Sheracy followed Angus Reach's approach to investigative journalism. His series on 'The White Slaves of England' were published in *Pearson's Magazine*, a popular illustrated journal which was sold in parts which could then be bound together to form thick morocco-bound half-yearly volumes.

'Leeds can hardly be termed a picturesque city' wrote Tom Bradley in 1893. How right he was, for now its surrounding fields were all choked with factories and worker's houses, from which thousands of coal fires belched out a dense mass of black sulphrous smoke. The evidence of the City Museum's sunshine records proved than it cut out one third of the light that fell in the cleaner northern suburbs. This illustration of 'The Industrial Aspect of Leeds from Richmond Hill' comes from The Graphic *of 18 July 1885.*

This photograph provides graphic evidence of the poor state of worker's housing in central Leeds. It shows the narrow yards to the north of Templar Street in the Leylands area. Note the back-to-back houses on the left, the two privies in the foreground and four in the distance, and the high walls of Hope Street Mills on the right.

Sheracy, R. 'The White Slaves of England: The Slipper-makers and Tailors of Leeds *Pearson's Magazine* II (1896) pp.263-8.

In the one downstairs room of a house in one of the lowest neighbourhoods in Leeds, I found an old slipper-maker at his tea. Although it was then past ten at night, his five little children were up and with him. As his wife explained:

'They've got to be there, when there's something to eat going. Father chucks them a bit of bread now and again, and so they likes to be there'.

It was a crowded scene, and one wondererd how a man could live and work in such a room. Yet here this man had worked for thirty years, and never less than fourteen hours a day. "Many a week", he said, "I have to work on Sundays also". Most of Saturday is wasted, as on Saturdays he has to carry the week's work to the shop, to have it inspected and paid for. He declared that his life was a miserable one, and that the trade had never been worse. "Work my very best, I can't earn 4d. an hour". It was a good week with him when he earned 18s, and out of this he had to pay 2s 8d. for rent, and 9d a week for findings. These findings would consist of paste (1½d), hemp (6d), sandpaper, ink and white wax (1½d). He was a man naturally of a jovial temperament, which only made his misery show more lamentably. He showed me a neat pair of patent leather slippers which he had just finished. "There's craft in that shoe; there's artisanship, there's work. We put 14d work of work in for 9d, to see if we can't win the trade back". And he added that he had spent two hours thirty minutes in making these slippers. He would receive 9d for this work. The slippers would be sold at retail for 3s. He laughed when I asked him what pleasure he enjoyed in life. "There's no such thing as pleasure for me. I go from my bed to my seat, and from my seat to my bed, though now and again I may get, say, an hour over my paper". He laughed again when I asked him if he was able to save anything. "Not a blessed halfpenny", he said; and his wife added that she could never make out how they managed to get along on his wages. She did the baking, and home baking was a comfortable thing. Some weeks she might get about 3d worth of meat for the family dinner, but that was not often. Bread and tea was what they mainly lived on, and plenty of "working man's beef — "that is to say onions". "There's grand stuff in onions", said this cheerful yet most unhappy man, who, in conclusion, told me that he meant to go on working his hardest until he could work no more, and that then, he supposed, they would find room for him in the workhouse . . .

I visited the club of the Jewish Tailors' Union, in Regent Street, in the notorious Leylands, a club which occupies a room which was once a Baptist chapel. I endeavoured to obtain information from various members, but their prudence was extreme. They were all very comfortable, they said, earning splendid wages, and they mentioned as their weekly earnings sums which they did not obtain in a month. Rumours of anti-Jewish immigration laws have disturbed them, and they do not know what to say. But from what I saw in the sweating dens in the Leylands, I am convinced that their circumstances are at least as bad as those of the sweated tailors in London. They all work on a weekly wage, and from twelve to seventeen hours a day. Here may be seen, in some filthy room in an old dilapidated factory in the Leylands, fifty people (men, women, boys and girls), all huddled together, sewing as though for dear life. A girl may be earning 6s a week, a man from 22s to 30s. The stench in the room, its uncleanliness, surpass description. The finished garments are lying pell-mell on the floor in the filth and vermin. They are "flogged into their work" as one said, "for all the time the gaunt sweater stalks about, scolding, inspecting, while now and then he will snatch a garment from some worker's hand, and set himself to work upon it, whilst a stream of vituperation pours from his lips. He is usually a haggard and starving man, himself a victim of inhuman competition. There are weeks when he does not earn a penny for himself. In a good week he may earn £10 . . .

A girl whom I interviewed at the office of the Wholesale Clothiers' Operatives Union, told me that she had often spent 10d on sewings out of a weekly earning of 2s 7d. She remembered one week when she had only earned a shilling,

and had had to pay 8d. She had given up tailoring in despair, as she could not make a living at it. She had been in a "punishing house", and had often been so weak from want of food that she had fainted over her machine. Many of her fellow workers used to beg food off the men in the factory, but she had never cared to do this, as it led to things.

The girls have to pay a 1d, or 2d, a week "for cook", that is to say, for having the food they bring with them warmed up. The tax is compulsory, though many of the girls never use the dining-room, for the reason that the dining-room is often so small that but a small proportion of the girls can be accommodated. I met one girl who had paid 2d a week "for cook" for ten years without every going into the dining room.

Fines are everywhere inflicted. Miss Ford said about them: "Unfortunately, thanks to the Judges' interpretation of the Truck Act, these are legal". She mentioned the case of a girl who had to pay a fine of 2d when her day's earning were 1½d. This was for being a minute late. The fines are registered by a timekeeper, who is usually a boy and who gets a commission on the total amount. The fines for bad work are very heavy. I spoke to a woman who told me that a week or two previous 2s had been deducted from her week's

These drawings were made in a Leeds tailoring sweatshop by Pillard in the mid-1890s to illustrate Robert Sheracy's articles on 'The White Slaves of England'. They show the girls at their sewing benches in a Leylands 'sweating den', and waiting, unpaid, while their work arrived.

earnings of 4s 2d for bad work. The bad work in question had afterwards been sold as good work, but the 2s were never refunded.

The wages are further reduced by one-twelfth (1d in the 1s) for steam power, and if a girl takes the work home she pays the 1d. in the 1s all the same. At one punishing-house in Leeds the girls each pay a proportion of the rent of the factory, besides the toll of power. The masters like the wages to be round sums, and odd pennies are confiscated on the promise of a trip for the girls. "But we never get no trip", said my informant.

Subject as it is to all these fines, tolls, and roundings-off, the maximum wage of 15s a week (which can only be earned by the best workers, working full time and even overtime) is generally reduced below 12s. In the slack season many girls cannot earn more than 2s. a week. I spoke to a machine hand who told me that for months together she had not earned above 10d a week during the slack season.

Masters take advantage of the girls' want to beat down the prices per piece at this time. "One time, when we were all very hungry", she said, "the foreman told us there were 400 sailor suits coming up. Would we do them at 3d each? We refused, as the lowest price was 3½d. each. The foreman kept us waiting a day and a half, and at last we were so hungry that we gave in".

"The masters often say", said another woman "We have so many hundred articles to be sewn, if you like to do them at such a reduced rate". We prefer not to be idle, and accept, expecting to have so many to sew. But the masters had lied, and there is very much less to sew than had been promised".

The brutality of the foremen is much complained of by the girls. "If he can bully, he is a good foreman". In some houses very foul language is used towards the girls. The girls are never informed when work is slack. They come to the factory, and have to remain there doing nothing. This is to prevent people knowing that the factory is slack.

A machine girl described her experiences in this respect to me; "I come in at 8am. If I'm late I'll be fined 1d or 2d. There will be nothing for me to do. Then I'll sit at my machine doing nothing till half-past twelve. Then I'll ask the foreman if I may go home. He'll say: "No, there's orders coming up after dinner". Dinner? I probably haven't any, knowing work was slack and expecting to get home. So I go without it. At half-past one, I'll go back to my machine and sit doing nothing. Foreman will say: "Work hasn't come up yet". I have to sit at my machine.

"Once I fainted from hunger, and asked to be allowed to go home, but they wouldn't let me, and locked me up in the dining-room. I sit at my machine till 3 or 4. Then the foreman will say, as though he were conferring a favour: "The orders don't seem to be coming in, you can go home till the morning". And I go home without having earned a farthing. Sometimes work may come in the afternoon, and then I will stay on till 6.30, earning wage for the last two or three hours".

1902

Sir Henry Rider Haggard (1856-1925) is best remembered today as the author of *She, King Solomon's Mines* and *Montezuma's Daughter*. Most of his non fictional work lay in the area of agriculture, farmers and labourers, and it was for this that he received his knighthood in 1912.
H.Rider Haggard. *Rural England* (London 1902) II 303

Being not at all well at the time, I asked to be directed to the quietest hotel in Leeds. If that hostelry was the most quiet, what the others can be like I know not. All night long trams ran, engines shrieked, and carts rattled in a fashion that made sleep almost impossible. Never have I visited a city that was noisier, or one more busy and thriving.

1903

This was Colonel Harding's speech at the formal presentation of the City Square statuary to the City of Leeds. After the ceremony among the crowds in City Square, the Colonel's great generosity was recognised by the granting of the freedom of the city.
Leeds Mercury, 17 September 1903.

"The reception which you have given me today in this historic hall, where I have attended many great meetings as a humble spectator, the generosity of the references which have been made to me in the public Press, the letters which I have received from many correspondents, the great honour that has been done me by my colleagues in the city council today — all this makes it difficult for me adequately to express to you my thanks.

"You have referred with much too great a kindness to what you were good enough to call the services in various directions I have rendered to the City of Leeds. I have done my best. But I am conscious that many of us have done the same, each within the limits of his leisure, his means, and his abilities for all that was good for the religious, philanthropic, and educational welfare of the people of Leeds.

"The only difference, perhaps, is that the work which we have inaugurated today is in a somewhat new direction. In the nature of it, it is somewhat obtrusive, it has attracted public attention. But for that, I feel I have done no more than many distinguished citizens, some of whom are amongst us today, have done, and I hope the city of Leeds will always gather round it men who will know how to do their duty, men who will consider it a privilege to serve their city.

"Seven years ago, shortly after the corporation had come into possession of the site of the Old Cloth Hall (on which, I think, we need not waste artistic regrets), and when the ground was still in a chaotic condition, and without form and void, I was in Italy, and I read in a local paper that there was a proposal to erect in the middle of it, or underneath it, a lavatory or a tramway waiting room — admirable things in their way, which appealed so much to the ratepayers. It occurred to me, however, that it was inadvisable to do these things, or any others, until the Corporation had first settled upon some plan on which to deal, step by step, with this important site, a site certainly the most important in Leeds, because it is that into which streams pour from the railways.

"I amused myself in my leisure in Italy in making a little plan of what I considered might possibly be done with this site; and I sent it to my friend, Mr Bakewell, architect, and asked him to put it into form. Much to my surprise, the Corporation did me the great honour of accepting this plan; and being anxious that it should be fully carried out, I was not conscious in offering certain monuments that I did anything which required the magnificent thanks you have bestowed upon me today. I was rather conscious of the tremendous responsibility I was undertaking in carrying out this great art matter . . .

"What I have done is in the nature of an experiment. Of isolated monuments there are plenty throughout the country, both in London and the provinces-monuments of men who rendered great national and local service. Some of them have

By the end of the Victorian period a number of influential industrialists and their families were beginning to effect a significant number of improvements in the appearance of Leeds and in the life of its people. One of these, Col W.T.Harding, conceived the idea of a City Square, and finally completed this project by presenting its centrepiece, the Black Prince by Sir Thomas Brock. Here we see the presentation taking place on 16 September 1903.

proved to be works of great artisitc merit, and others possibly have not proved to be works of art. But more or less they were all of a utilitarian kind after all, and only form a secondary point of view where they considered as works of art.

We have been attempting today to bring decorative art works as such among the people, and surely such works have not been much in evidence in this country, not even in London. The delightful fountain of Mr Gilbert in Piccadilly-circus, is however, an example; and I know quite well that there are many persons who think that works of that kind — works, for instance, like Mr Drury's beautiful figures in City Square — are quite out of character in a business place and in a dirty place like Leeds. It is time that they apply to Leeds the description in Solomon's Song, it is "black but comely"; perhaps it would be better to speak of Leeds as comely, but, alas! black — and one of the difficulties we shall have to contend with now will be to maintain it in something like good order.

I am not very sure of the experiment we are going to try of maintaining in good condition the monuments which have been put up, because as a general rule, even in London, when once a monument is put up, the thing is left then to the fate for evermore. We are trying an interesting experiment of — if possible in a dirty place like Leeds — maintaining them in an artistic way, and if we succeed, we shall have rendered service not only to our own town, but to many of the provincial towns.

I do not agree that works of decorative art as such are wasted in business places. It is with communities just as it is with individuals. An individual may quite properly devote himself heart and soul to his business or his profession; yet, after all, a man of culture is a man who surely devotes part of his leisure to matters entirely unconnected with money making, matters connected, say, with science, art or music. So with our great cities. Let us by all means be proud of our great factories and workshops, and our great and varied industries, but let us, then, be able to rise above the sordid, and rejoice in the beautiful . . .

1905

George Bernard Shaw (1856-1950), the great Irish dramatist, was well known for his strongly-held, controversial, and brilliantly expressed views. While in Leeds his hosts took him for a ride on the top of a Kirkstall tram, when he praised the rows of back-to-back houses. He thought that the practice of hanging washing across the streets was excellent since it was likely to raise the standard of wearing apparel!

Leeds Mercury 15 February 1905, account of George Bernard Shaw's lecture "What is the use of an Arts Club"?, at the invitation of Leeds Arts Club, at Leeds Philosophical Hall:

"Art is a thing that can finally make you believe that Leeds as it exists at present is a very intolerable place, that it is a place that no decent individual ought to live, and that you individually have no right to be alive at all. It even has the power, finally, of driving you, under certain provocation, to burn down your town — and you might do worse, you know, although Leeds is a very much better town than many I have been in. Now that I come to think of it, the use of an Arts Club in Leeds might be to make you burn down the town and to replace it with a better one. But in order to do that I am afraid it would be necessary to get rid of the people of Leeds, and replace them with a rather different sort of people."

Index